JESUS AND THE EUCHARIST

JESUS
AND
THE
EUCHARIST

Tad W. Guzie, S.J.

PAULIST PRESS

New York   Paramus, N.J.   Toronto

Copyright © 1974 by Tad W. Guzie, S.J. Book design by Paula Wiener. Cover design
by Morris Berman. Library of Congress Catalog Card Number: 73-90069. ISBN:
0-8091-1858-0. Published by Paulist Press: *Editorial Office:* 1865 Broadway, New
York, N.Y. 10023. *Business Office:* 400 Sette Drive, Paramus, N.J. 07652. Printed and
bound in the United States of America. Imprimi potest: Bruce F. Biever, S.J., August 3,
1973; nihil obstat: Richard J. Sklba, S.S.L., S.T.D., September 14, 1973; imprimatur:
William E. Cousins, Archbishop of Milwaukee, September 19, 1973. The nihil obstat
and imprimatur are a declaration that a book or pamphlet is considered to be free from
doctrinal or moral error. It is not implied that those who have granted the nihil
obstat and imprimatur agree with the contents, opinions, or statements expressed.

Contents

Preface 1

1 Flights into Magic 3

2 Two Questions About Reality 24

3 The Last Supper and the Eucharist 42

4 The Bread and Wine 60

5 The Cross and the Eucharist 75

6 Symbol Upon Symbol 103

7 From Magic to Mystery 128

8 Sacrifice 145

Preface

The real Jesus took real bread and wine and identified himself with it.

This is one very simple way of stating how it all began. More has to be said about the setting in which this action took place, the religious meaning of what Jesus did, how his followers understood it. But the fact remains that we start with a remarkably simple ritual gesture done by a man who was facing death. And just as the man's death was to affect the way millions of people would live, so his gesture at that last meal shaped the way they would worship. Millions and millions of people. There lies the problem. When untold numbers of people, spread over twenty centuries and coming from cultural backgrounds numbering many times twenty, repeat a ritual action which originated outside their own time and culture, it would be amazing if the simplicity of the first gesture were to remain untouched. For that matter it would be amazing if the real Jesus remained untouched.

The theology of the sacraments has usually been handled quite separately from christology, the question of Jesus. But it has been my experience that the kind of questions asked today by college students, religious educators and interested adults makes it important to link these two areas of theology very closely. People's questions have to do with the meaning of Jesus and all the symbols we use to interpret his meaning, both in our worship and in our religious language generally. In our search for the meaning of christian ideas, we have become quite used to the concept that the Old Testament is the dictionary used by the writers of the New; and so we look back at the religious ideas and practices of judaism for the roots of christian ideas. But analytical psychology and other modern sciences of man have made it clear that we must look much further than this, particularly when we are dealing with ritual. Ritual symbols emerge from man's consciousness, at the very dawn of human history, as his most fundamental way of getting hold of the world he lives in. The most basic symbols we use, both in our interpretations of Jesus and in the sacraments that celebrate his mystery, originate entirely outside the Bible.

I have therefore paid much attention to basic questions regarding man's religious imagination. How do our minds meet reality, and how do we ask the God-question at different stages of our development? To what kind of question are rituals and sacraments an answer? How does our religious understanding develop, both historically and in our personal lives? Answers to these questions shed much light on changing interpretations of the eucharist and changing attitudes toward the person of Jesus over the course of two millennia.

Many of the books mentioned in the notes were selected because they are non-technical works of sound scholarship which the reader may find useful for further pursuit of an idea. Biblical quotations throughout the book are taken from *The Jerusalem Bible*.

Marquette University
Pentecost, 1973

1

Flights into Magic

JESUS' LAST SUPPER with his friends was an event, a fact. But important facts are always interpreted. The ritual action that took place at that meal has been interpreted with a variety of concepts and images. It is eucharist, thanksgiving, it is the new passover meal, a representation of the sacrifice of Calvary, a sacrificial meal, communion with God. So for Jesus, who has been understood in an equal variety of ways. He was a man who died, and for those who did not believe in him it all stopped there. His death was a fact, and the fact had no special meaning. But those who believed in him, who underwent the experiences we call easter and pentecost, interpreted his death and his whole life right back to his birth. The first christians saw Jesus as the second Adam, the new Moses, the true high priest, the word become flesh, the cosmic Christ in whom all of creation would be restored. All these images were ways of spelling out the meaning of who Jesus is for us.

Once we get used to interpretations of an event, it is not at all easy to remember that the event and the interpretation are not the same thing. The one cannot simply by identified with the other. Interpretation begins as an effort to unfold the meaning of an event. But as the process of interpretation continues, it is not always controlled. Like a stone wrapped in a snowball and sent rolling down a snow-covered bank, the event can get so wrapped in interpretations, one layer added to another, that there is sometimes little relationship between the last layer and the first fact lying somewhere inside.

The real Jesus took real bread and wine and identified himself with it.

This event, sent rolling down the bank of christian history, has undergone more interpretations than any other incident in Jesus' life. By no means have the interpretations always conflicted. New passover, sacrificial meal, communion with the body of Christ: these ideas all originally complemented one another, each in its own way illuminating some facet of the Lord's supper and its meaning for us. But gradually interpretation was laid upon interpretation. And eventually interpretation came to conflict with interpretation, particularly at the time of the reformation, when understanding of the eucharist became one of the chief issues dividing christians. When one is dealing with, let us say, the tenth or eleventh layers of interpretation (which is roughly the state of things by the time the eucharistic question is formulated in concepts like "real presence" and "transubstantiation"), it is not always an easy matter to see how the interpretations relate to the original event.

It is not just theologians who engage in the business of interpretation. Popular piety has always had a hand in it, and a strong case can be made for saying that popular interpretation has had a more potent influence on the development of christian thought than have theologians. Popular piety embodies a living faith, a lived understanding of faith—and indeed the earliest interpretations of Jesus were not devised by trained theologians. Theologians come along and lay out that lived understanding in disciplined statements, which then feed back into popular piety, and the dialectic begins anew. This is basically how we get the phenomenon of interpretation laid upon interpretation.

In the realm of *ritual*, history indicates that theologians seem to have exercised much less control over the interpretative process than elsewhere. Perhaps this is because theologians have usually been more interested in manipulating ideas, frequently very abstract ones, than in dealing with the maze of concrete behavioral and artistic expressions of faith which we find in rituals like the ritual of the mass. However this may be, the development of christian ritual has been strongly influenced by popular understanding of Jesus and his mystery. Theologians have on the whole intervened only when popular developments have gotten completely out of hand.

The result of all this is that religious rituals tend to deteriorate, to lose their original sense and take on superstitious and magical meanings. Jesus' simple gesture with bread and wine was repeated with equal simplicity when the first christians "met in their homes for the breaking of bread" (Acts 2:46). Incredibly enough, medieval christians were repeating basically the same ritual when they paid priests to hold the host up longer after the consecration, in the belief that so long as the host was elevated, sins were being forgiven and souls released from purgatory. Examples of ritual's tendency to decay into magic are not lacking today. It would be difficult to find so gross an understanding of the eucharist as the one just mentioned, but there is still a good touch of superstition wrapped up in many people's view of that ritual.

Popular piety has also affected the way Jesus himself has been interpreted. Some interpretations of him do not relate to anything like a real person who was "tempted in every way that we are" (Heb 4:15). The trouble here seems to come from the wrong kind of insistence on the classical formula "Jesus Christ is truly God." This is only a half-truth, and half-truths are not really true. One who wants to be faithful to christian orthodoxy cannot insist on the first half of this dogma of Chalcedon without affirming and equally emphasizing the second half. "The same Jesus Christ is truly man." If anything, the bishops of Chalcedon were more concerned with Jesus' manhood, because the immediate occasion for this council was Eutyches' denial of Christ's full humanity. Taken in its historical context, that dogma is telling us that whatever we say about Jesus' divinity cannot *conflict* with the humanity of the carpenter's son. We know his divinity only *in* his humanity; and whatever we say about him as God can be truthfully said only when we start with a real person who lived our human condition and died in it. The dogma formulates, in a particular historical and philosophical setting, the core of christian belief that had already been clearly stated in the less philosophical language and imagery used by the New Testament writers. Jesus is God's final and decisive word to man (Heb 1:2), the unique mediator between God and mankind, himself a man (1 Tim 2:5). The dogma talks about Jesus' relationship to us and to God. It does *not* talk about Jesus' self-awareness, his growth as a human personality, or his own personal experience of the human condition.[1]

But popular understanding of the dogma has applied it to Jesus' personal psychology. There are few christians who (along with the church fathers themselves) have not fallen into the trap of thinking of Jesus as one who played out a script written by the Father—a script which, thanks to his divinity, he knew and understood well in advance, including how it would all end. We see a haloed Jesus with his friends gathered around him at table, a Jesus who is already virtually risen, in total control of history, including his own. He has a rough three days ahead of him. But again, thanks to his divinity, he already has all the answers. There is one sacrament he has not yet "instituted" (traditional language often reinforces the know-it-all Jesus), and so for history's sake he goes on to institute it.

This language sounds flippant, but I do not think it is a complete caricature of the popular view of Jesus at the last supper. It is a view that one can easily enough come away with from the scriptural accounts of the event, which read an easter understanding of Jesus back into his historical life. It is also a view that has been fostered by artists. One need only think of Da Vinci's or Dali's paintings of the last supper, which likewise embody an easter understanding of the event. Or there is the print I saw some years ago, where a haloed Christ is distributing round white wafers to kneeling apostles, who (good catholics that they are) receive the host on their tongues.

The latter example is historically ludicrous, but it should make us aware of the fact that our faith imagery does not necessarily correspond to the original event. There is nothing wrong in itself with faith-interpretation so long as it is understood precisely *as interpretation*. If we allow the interpretation to become totally identified with the event, we are bound to end up with a view that places both Jesus and the last supper outside the human condition, outside life and the experience of death. Interpretation, even the most creative and edifying kind of faith-interpretation, must never be allowed to cloud over the fact that Jesus was a person who experienced the human condition *as we experience it*.[2] The story of the agony in the garden implies that acceptance of death was, to say the least, a real struggle for him. In the Letter to the Hebrews, we read that Jesus submitted so humbly that his prayer to be rescued from death *was heard* (Heb 5:7). The gospel writers indicate that he prayed as any genuinely pious man would pray in the face of death: he prayed that the bitter chalice would *pass him by* (Mt 26:39).

The point is that his victory over death, and the answer to his prayer to be rescued from death, came in a way unforeseen by him (as answers to prayer usually come to us as well). This point is often muddled by popular understanding, which implies that the only reason why Jesus did not in fact use his divine powers to come down from the cross was that the moment was not yet ripe, and he *knew* just how he would be vindicated. In short, though he believed in God's absolute faithfulness to him, Jesus could not have known the outcome of his struggle with death unless he were exempted from the human condition. Whatever he did at the last supper, he did with an awareness of his impending death; and his awareness included all the human uncertainties regarding death. To the extent that interpretation lets us forget this point, we are bound to misunderstand the connection between the eucharist and the death of a man. There is a kind of liturgical triumphalism which emphasizes the risen Christ at the cost of the real Jesus who experienced death as we do, and which therefore pulls both the Lord and his supper outside the human condition.

In all of this one can see a tendency toward magic. Magic involves an attitude which does not take finite reality seriously. Magic deals with supra-human means of escaping from or overcoming the human condition; it does not deal *with* the human condition. Christian faith refuses magic. It does so in its insistence that we are to find and understand the transcendent, the world of God, in the man Jesus who remains finite even as the first-born from among the dead. This is what is meant by saying that Jesus Christ is truly God *and* truly man. But religious interpretation can easily degenerate into a magical attitude, and christian interpretation is no exception. This is the phenomenon we have been looking at. Just as the original meaning of the last supper has often deteriorated into a magical meaning, so has the real Jesus sometimes been all but obscured by a magical Jesus, a Jesus who in the last analysis stands outside humanity. In both cases interpretation, which is initially meant to unfold the meaning of real events and persons, has carried believers in the direction of an escape *from* the human condition rather than a confrontation *with* it.

Why should religious interpretation lead to the unreal, the magical, the superstitious? To answer this question, we have to take a closer look at how the process of religious interpretation works, and specifically how it has worked in the history of christianity. This process has to be understood if we are to distinguish layers of interpretation and come to understand the tradition we have inherited. The following pages will trace the way the magical Jesus and the magical eucharist, both still very much with us, have come about. This is a rather negative way of getting at how the process of religious interpretation works; but unreal interpretations of the person in whom we believe should be brought to light and set aside before we go any further.

***

Christianity has been most reluctant in recent centuries to expose itself to comparison with other religions. This is certainly true of preaching and catechetics, even today. Few people have heard anything in the course of their religious instruction about the similarities between christian doctrines and the teachings of other world religions. Christians believe in a transcendent reality who is also immanent in human hearts, a reality who is supreme beauty and love, mercy and compassion. They believe that the way to him is repentance, self-denial, prayer, love of one's neighbor and even of one's enemies. They believe that only the love of God will bring happiness, and they understand ultimate happiness as knowledge of God and union with him. But most christians are unaware (or sometimes unwilling to accept) that the very *same* beliefs I have just mentioned are found in world religions such as judaism, islam, hinduism, buddhism, taoism.[3]

Prior to the modern age, faith in God and the teachings of the church were very much at the center of man's interpretation of reality. As it saw that world falling apart, the christian church felt an almost compulsive need to defend itself and its traditions against the onslaught of what we now call secularization—a man-oriented rather than God-oriented interpretation of reality and human experience. This resulted in an uncritical emphasis on christianity's uniqueness. Its points of contact with non-christian forms of religious interpretation were largely unknown or ignored. The expert in comparative religions who demonstrated these points of contact was, if not heretical, at least highly suspect and certainly very threatening.

This has not always been the case. We should recall that it took a generation or two for christianity to separate itself decisively from judaism. Paul's insistence that gentile converts not be held to the practices of the old law would have influenced this eventual separation. But opposition to the followers of Jesus developed only gradually, and it is not until the decade of the eighties that we find an organized effort to force the christian jews out of the synagogues. In the meantime, they saw no difficulty in attending the jewish services they had always attended.

Was Jesus himself aware that he was founding a new religion? Scholars have argued whether Jesus was conscious of being the messiah. One must not of course put too much emphasis on a term. In Jesus' day "messiah" was a particularly troublesome term because in its popular sense it suggested a political savior, and Jesus certainly did not see himself in this role. In any case, we define our identities according to the many roles we play, and no single word is ever going to express anyone's total self-definition. This is one reason why the gospels use so many different titles to unfold the meaning of Jesus.

Apart from the question of terms and of what titles Jesus himself would have used to describe his role, there are few current scholars who would not agree that Jesus saw himself as a decisive person— decisive for the kingdom of God and therefore decisive for judaism. Otherwise too many things in the gospels would simply make no sense, even if we allow for the great amount of post-resurrection understanding which the gospels read back into Jesus' historical life. His attacks against the Torah and his deliberate violations of the sabbath laws make sense only if Jesus possessed a mature awareness of his own authority. The same holds true for the events at the end of his life. Jesus went up to Jerusalem fully aware that death awaited him there. His acceptance of death is indicated in the prayer of Gethsemane; and the *nature* of this acceptance, the terms in which he saw his impending death, is spelled out in the ritual gesture with bread and wine at the last supper. That gesture would make no sense unless he consciously attached a messianic significance to his death, a significance having to do with the whole idea of the kingdom he had been preaching. Bread and wine, as we shall see later, already had a messianic meaning in the desert communities.

But for all this, I believe it would be severely anachronistic to say that Jesus thought of himself as the "founder of a new religion," with all that this phrase connotes to modern man. The judaism of Jesus' day was made up of many schools and sects; there is no reason to think that either Jesus or his first followers saw themselves as anything but faithful jews trying to penetrate the true meaning of God's revelation as it was embodied in the history of the hebrew people.

As the gospel spread to the greco-roman world at large, that world found christian teachings to be rather odd—but for quite different reasons from those which led to jewish rejection of the new message. The jews had trouble with a few essential points like faith in a man who was obviously dead, and a man who had taught his followers to play it so free and easy with the observances of the law. The gentile world had quite other problems, because belief in Christ looked so little like their own religions. A century after Jesus' time we find a writer like Justin Martyr (a greek philosopher who became a christian and founded a school in Rome) pointing out that christian ideas about Jesus are not really so different as his readers may think. When christians talk about Jesus Christ who was crucified and died and rose again, "we propose nothing different from what you believe regarding those whom you consider sons of Jupiter." Justin goes on to show how, for christians, Jesus is the son of God in a unique way; but first he is interested in striking similarities.

If we assert that the Word of God was born of God in a special way, different from ordinary births, this should be no extraordinary thing to you, who say that Mercury is the angelic Word of God. And if anyone objects that Jesus was crucified [i.e. arguing that gods are not subject to death], in this too he is on a par with those reputed sons of Jupiter of yours who suffered [Aesculapius, Bacchus, Hercules, etc.]. When we affirm that he was born of a virgin, understand this in connection with what you say about Perseus. And when we say that he cured the lame, the paralytic and those born blind, we seem to be talking about deeds very similar to those which Aesculapius is supposed to have done.[4]

Not many pastors would be prepared to try out a comparison like that on their sunday congregations. There is more to be said of course; someone like Irenaeus, writing shortly after Justin, does a detailed analysis of the vast differences between christian teaching and the cosmic myths. Still, in our preaching and catechetics today, we have not yet come to terms with the important historical *fact* that ideas like divine sonship, a god who dies and rises, miracles as proof of divine power, and virgin birth were well known long before christianity came along. Such ideas, as the study of history and culture and psychology shows, belong to a whole category of ancient ideas and symbols which express man's eternal hopes. It was only natural that if such ideas *are* radical symbols, rooted in the mind of man, they would have been applied to Jesus and used to express faith in Jesus as the one who fulfills man's hopes.[5]

Like the hero-gods of antiquity who conquered the powers of evil and who are frequently shown conquering dragons, Jesus is seen as one who vanquishes the powers of death and darkness. All of the church fathers' imagery regarding Christ's victory over Satan is very much in line with ancient mythology. Both Christ and Orpheus (to choose only one of the many god-men of antiquity) were men who became mediators of the divine, a role which both religions symbolize in the image of a good shepherd. The notion of a cosmic man— one who stands at the beginning of life, or who represents the final goal of life and creation—is found under different names and personifications in China, India, ancient Persia. Paul is by no means using an original image when he develops the parallels and contrasts between Adam and Christ, the first and last cosmic men.

Many god-heroes undergo death and rebirth, or achieve the reward of immortality through their sufferings. Justin chose examples only from greco-roman religion. The same process of death and rebirth is emphasized in ancient rituals of initiation which identify the worshiper with the life of the god. John is not being original when he interprets the christian initiation of baptism as a "rebirth" (Jn 3). Nor is Paul when he interprets it, even more vividly, as a ritual in which we "go into the tomb with Christ and join him in death so that we might live a new life" (Rom 6:4). In the ancient world and in primitive cultures today, initiation rituals often take place at various stages in one's life, defining the passage from one stage to the next. This idea too is built into man's psyche, and it is articulated in any religion that provides special rites at the time of birth, marriage or death. In moving the sacrament of confirmation from the middle years of grade school to a time when young people are more capable of personal commitment to an adult faith, recent catholic practice is only affirming our radical need for appropriate "rites of passage." The same need and symbolism is at work in the passover rite, commemorating the hebrews' passage from Egypt to the promised land, from slavery to freedom, death to life. Jesus himself, as the first christians saw it, "passed over" from this world to the father (Jn 13:1).

But the first christians also emphasized that this latter event was a once-and-for-all event. Christianity is an historical and future-oriented religion, not a cyclical one. It looks back to the death and resurrection of Jesus as an event which is decisive for all time, making it possible for us to look forward to final union with a transcendent God. The christian is not to identify himself with the cycle of nature, personified in the stories of Orpheus and other god-heroes of antiquity—an eternally repeated cycle of birth, growth, death, rebirth. So for the first christians any ritual had to be a commemoration of Jesus' death and resurrection with the explicit purpose of expressing their future hope. But once the persecutions were over and christianity entered the mainstream of hellenistic culture, the church began incorporating ideas from the cyclical religions. A liturgical year was gradually built up, cyclically recalling the events of Jesus' life and ministry, beginning with his birth. Today we take all this for granted. But to appreciate the significance of this evolution and the potential impact of bringing back the old in order to interpret the new, we need only recall that the apostle Paul never even thought it worthwhile to talk about any of the events in Jesus' life and ministry except his death and resurrection.

Later on we shall look more closely at the development of symbolism in christian ritual, its values and its aberrations. The point I want to emphasize here is one that is much too easily overlooked, and we overlook it constantly in our effort to defend the uniqueness of christianity. Christian teaching insists that *Jesus* is unique; nowhere does it say that the *process of interpreting him* is unique. In the same way, although christianity is not a cyclical religion, it has nonetheless brought in many symbolic elements from such religions. There is nothing intrinsically wrong with this. The problem arises— and it is a problem we cannot even recognize unless we watch for the profound similarities between christianity and other religions—when the process of interpretation comes to obscure what *is* distinctive about christianity, namely the person of Jesus. This has happened many times in the course of christian history, and it began happening even before the first century was over.

Trouble was inevitable because the tools of interpretation which the biblical writers along with the ancients used were tools which could be indiscriminately applied to any type of reality. Imagination and storytelling were the basic tools, and they could be applied to transcendental ideas and historical realities, to creations and projections of the mind as well as to events in the world of history. Ideas and events: the two categories are not alike. But the mythological imagination handles them both, without distinguishing between them.

Myths, which are simply stories embodying some truth about the world, explain mysterious ultimates like the origin of the universe, or of good and evil. Today we get our models or images for interpreting the universe from the empirical sciences, from technology, from sophisticated psychological and sociological theories. For the ancients, the meaning of the universe was spelled out in stories about the gods. The world of Olympus, the doings of the gods *before time began*, made up a world of archetypal models which provided an explanation for the things that happen in *this* world, which imitates what goes on or went on in the heavenly primordial world. These ancient myths are by no means arbitrary; they very accurately project man's most basic experiences of reality and human relationships. The writer of Genesis shows no interest in what happened in the heavenly world before time began, but he uses the same kind of archetypal myth in his stories about the origin of the universe, the entry of sin into the world, and the breakdown of the relationship between God and man.

Myths are therefore also used to interpret events that happen *in history*—and this not just in the ancient world. Stories are told about great men and events precisely in order to concretize their greatness, to give flesh and blood to what otherwise might remain bare bones in the popular mind. George Washington and the events of World War II have been just as susceptible to this kind of mythologizing as Abraham, the exodus, or Jesus. Such stories are selective in their details; they do not recount the whole event. They heighten a man's greatness; and if his weaknesses appear in the story, they are there to show how he overcame the weakness (like George Washington and the cherry tree). Myths also involve composite figures and events. The french and russian revolutions were both long processes, with important events spread over a period of years. But myth centers many of the accomplishments of these revolutions around single events like the storming of the bastille in Paris or the winter palace in Leningrad—events which were not in themselves all that significant from a military point of view.

The gospels are filled with this type of myth. The sermon on the mount is a composite of Jesus' teaching, just as the accounts of his cures and miracles often conflate many events into a single story. The story of pentecost is another good example. Peter gets up and gives a rousing speech which cuts the people to the heart, and we are told that three thousand were baptized that day. It is quite unlikely that twelve men could accomplish that feat without a firehose. What the story does is to fuse into one day events and experiences which undoubtedly took place over a longer period of time in those exciting days after easter. Such stories are not untrue *unless* we try to make them something other than what they are: stories meant to stress the importance and meaning of a significant person or event.

This may all seem obvious to the reader who has had experience with literature, but it has not always been so obvious. Much of the modern conflict between science and religion stems from a misreading of biblical myths. People who would not dream of reading Shakespeare without a good historical dictionary are still unaware that the creation stories in Genesis have nothing to do with astronomy or evolution. There is a kind of defensiveness deep inside the religious mind that makes us want to read every story about Jesus as though it had appeared on the front page of a newspaper. Even after we have been informed that the biblical writers did not know that kind of reporting, and that the gospels belong more to the editorial page than to the front page, we are still afraid to recognize myths for what they are. We are afraid we are going to lose something.

The real loss comes when we look at the gospel stories as containing simply facts about Jesus and his life; for in this case, we are liable to miss the real fact, namely that the writer is trying to say something about the *meaning* of Jesus. If we take these stories as straightforward pieces of reporting and then go on to ask what the report means, the meaning we come up with is not necessarily going to square with the meaning intended by the writer. This happens of course in much preaching, and it is not a moral evil; such interpretation has fostered much faith. But sooner or later we have to recognize the fact that the scriptures are the normative writings of our faith not because of what we *think* they say, but because of what those writers *intended* to say. The modern age, with its critical methods in so many areas of knowledge, has taken us beyond the point where christianity can remain credible to an educated adult who is consistently given uncritical or merely pious explanations of scripture.

This explanation of mythical thinking has perhaps been unnecessarily long, especially since the importance of myth has been so emphasized by the scholarship of the last few decades, inside and outside the field of theology. But we are not at all finished with the job of clarifying the relationship of myth and imagination to our traditional dogmas. On the one hand, recognizing myth as a way of thinking, as a thoroughly symbolic way of talking about real things, constitutes a threat to much traditional theology and popular understanding of the faith. It has not been easy for catholic theology to abandon Adam as a single first man from whom the entire race got its biological origin; and it is interesting that theologians changed their minds on this point not because of the accumulation of archeological and *scientific* evidence to the contrary, but mainly because comparative *literary* study made the mythical genre of the Adam stories so evident. On the other hand, there is the tendency (stemming to some extent from Bultmann's program of demythologizing the gospel, and often involving much misunderstanding of Bultmann) which wants to do away with the historical events surrounding Jesus as decisive events in the history of man's relation with God. This tension is inevitable. It is not all that easy, even for biblical scholars, to sort out the interpretation of a biblical event from the event itself. As the last century of biblical scholarship has so forcefully taught us, we cannot write a biography of Jesus. And this brings us to the problem with mythical thinking as a tool of interpretation.

What is finite experience and what is not? What belongs to the world of meaning and what is historical fact? What belongs to the transcendent world and what has really taken place in our own? The mythical imagination does not distinguish. It interprets an event in the very act of reporting it, because it does not know how to report events *apart from* their meaning. It draws no line between event and interpretation and thus leaves an ambiguity. Who is the real Jesus and who is the mythologized Christ? Who is the real Jesus, and where is the dividing line between him and a Christ who might be interpreted beyond recognition? To the extent that mythical thinking operates in the gospels as a method of interpreting Jesus, these questions are not answered. For once the process of mythical interpretation goes into full operation, it can run on as it will; there is no built-in control over the process. Myth *can* give us the genuine meaning of an event or person. It can just as easily move us outside the world of history and finite experience into a world of pure meaning unrelated to real life, and ultimately into a world of magic.

Take for example the stories about Jesus' miracles. Such stories were common currency in the religious literature of the day. We saw the parallels which Justin Martyr drew between Jesus' cures and those of a greco-roman god; indeed, most of the hero-gods of ancient times were endowed with superhuman powers. We know too that the gospel stories are based on stories from the Old Testament: like the story of Elijah raising the widow's son to life (1 Kg 17:17-24), or that of Elisha reviving a dead child, or multiplying loaves so that people would have enough to eat (2 Kg 4:29-37, 42-44). People experienced Jesus as a healer, as one who presented the same prophetic credentials as Elijah or Elisha. His healing power very naturally came to be described in stories, myths, just like those told about Elijah or Elisha. If we come away from these stories with the impression of magical or superhuman medical powers, it is because we do not know how to distinguish a medical report from a myth. The gospel myths talk about Jesus' very *real* ability to heal in the same way that other great men have been healers. But what is real healing? The gospel writers knew that such stories were talking about the carpenter's son whose ultimate act of healing was to proclaim the forgiveness of sin (Mt 9:1-8; Mk 2:1-12; Lk 5:17-26). By subordinating the stories about physical cures to the healing which is forgiveness, the gospel writers place a control on the mythology of miracles. They introduce into a traditional form of storytelling a new element which is absent from the old stories about wonders worked by famous men or hero-gods.

It took the christian communities scattered around the mediterranean world a good century to filter out authentic interpretations of their faith from the unreal interpretations that were circulating at the same time. Today we know of gospels according to Matthew, Mark, Luke and John; second-century christians also knew of gospels according to the hebrews, the egyptians, Philip, Matthias, Peter and Thomas. We know of a single book called "Acts," the Acts of the Apostles; early christians were exposed to the Acts of John, of Paul, Peter, Andrew, Thomas and Philip. Some of these writings (the "apocrypha," writings which were not finally accepted as normative expressions of christian faith) are downright silly. The *Gospel of Thomas*, for instance, talks about the child Jesus making sparrows out of clay and turning them into living sparrows that fly. Another little boy who observes this wonder, and who runs to Joseph with the complaint that Jesus did it on a sabbath day, is struck dead in his tracks for his complaint. Jesus is not always such a vicious little brat in these writings, but most of the other stories about his childhood are equally absurd.

Some of the apocryphal writings are a great deal more sophisticated. The *Acts of John* describes a Jesus who isn't human at all. The writer, who gives himself the name of John the apostle, is called by a mature Jesus who is bald but full-bearded; his brother, who is with him at the same time, receives his call from one whom James perceives to be a child. The whole story is filled with different and conflicting physical perceptions of Jesus. The climax comes at the crucifixion when John runs away from Calvary and hides in a cave. Jesus appears to John there and tells him that it is all an act for the crowd's sake; he is only apparently being crucified. He then goes on to explain to John the symbolism of what is (not really) happening on Calvary. The cross, he says, is "sometimes called my word for your sakes, sometimes mind, sometimes Jesus, sometimes Christ, sometimes door, sometimes a way." The list goes on with a dozen other predicates attached to the cross: bread, seed, resurrection, Son, Father, Spirit, life, truth, faith, grace.

We know next to nothing about the century-long process whereby the rather small collection of writings now called the New Testament were sifted out from a vast body of texts, all claiming to be authentic expressions of christian faith. What we do know is that the sifting took place in the face of a strong tendency to do away with the real Jesus. All of these writings, both the accepted and the rejected ones, were interested in the meaning of Jesus, and all of them used myth. But *what* Jesus, and where *is* his meaning to be found? Many writings (I have given only a few extreme examples) attempted to explain his meaning by endowing him with incredible powers, or by presenting one who wasn't a man at all but God playing at being a man.

This latter approach really simplifies the whole thing. God is ultimate meaning. And if Jesus is plain and simply God, your problem of meaning is solved without having to mess about with the finite, and the fact of a man who died.

The same question keeps recurring. Nicaea and Chalcedon had to deal with attempts at philosophical expression which were not yet sufficiently nuanced, and which were unacceptable precisely because they diminished the reality of Jesus. The two councils thus made their contribution toward a christological "logic," a set of guidelines for speaking about Jesus within a particular philosophical frame of reference. But fed back into the popular religious imagination, notions like "Christ and the Father are of the same substance" or "Christ is truly God and truly man" easily become mythological. They acquire grossly inaccurate imaginative meanings. The progression of thought from the New Testament to the christological councils is an evolution from mythical thinking to logical thinking and the beginnings of philosophical expression. But the *logical* stage, once it is reached, cannot be *mythologized*. Mythical interpretation is as valid as the gospels themselves, but not when it is applied to the kind of logical definition which the conciliar fathers were searching for. What many christians take away from the doctrines of these councils bears very little resemblance to what the doctrines originally meant.

We are probably dealing here with a natural human tendency, for it is not at all easy to sustain the judeo-christian religious insight. The world surrounding the hebrews explained the universe, both human and divine, by appealing to a primordial world which is mirrored by the events of our finite world. Hebrew religious experience, on the other hand, insisted that God was to be found within history, within man's concrete experience. Christian faith came, asserting that God is to be found in the finite Jesus. But there is resistance to this type of faith. We all possess an innate desire for the human condition to be other than it is, and this desire seems easily to translate into a desire for the magical. The problem is further complicated by the fact that our most basic tool of religious interpretation—the mythical imagination—does not guarantee a hold on finite experience as the locus of *christian* faith.

***

All of this deeply affects the understanding of christian ritual. We have been looking at types of religious imagination which seek to interpret Jesus' meaning for faith by endowing him with superhuman powers and dispensing him in some way from full human experience of the finite. The same type of religious imagination has gone to work in the realm of ritual. James Joyce gives a classic expression of it in *A Portrait of the Artist as a Young Man*. Stephen, the young hero of the story, at one stage goes into a big religious fervor. His elaborate pious practices are noticed by his teachers, and one day the jesuit director calls him in and asks him if he has ever considered a vocation to the priesthood.

To receive that call, Stephen, said the priest, is the greatest honor that the Almighty God can bestow upon a man. No king or emperor on this earth has the power of the priest of God. No angel or archangel in heaven, no saint, not even the Blessed Virgin herself, has the power of a priest of God: the power of the keys, the power to bind and loose from sin, the power of exorcism, the power to cast out from the creatures of God the evil spirits that have power over them; the power, the authority, to make the great God of Heaven come down upon the altar and take the form of bread and wine. What an awful power, Stephen!

Stephen, we are told, "listened in reverent silence to the priest's appeal and through the words he heard even more distinctly a voice bidding him approach, offering him secret knowledge and secret power."[6] The boy has not misunderstood. Implicit in the director's words is a whole theology, familiar enough to catholics, which interprets the priestly ministry primarily in terms of power. Today, half a century after Joyce wrote, theology and catechetics emphasize the priesthood as ministry, as service to the christian community. But the concept of the "power to forgive" and the "power to consecrate" is usually still brought in somewhere as a key factor defining the priesthood.

The difficulty here is the same one we have been noting all along. Does such interpretation take the finite seriously? Most people will admit that it is stretching things a bit far to say that a man has the power to tell God what to do. Even if we exclude this exaggeration, what does it mean to say (as we often do) that a man has "power"

over finite elements like bread and wine? Is such interpretation necessary to explain the phenomenon of the eucharist? Is it even useful?
If the eucharist is to be a genuine memorial of the moment when the
real Jesus took real bread and wine and identified himself with it, to
what extent do the bread and wine have to become something other
than what they are?

Christian orthodoxy demands that whatever statements we make
about Jesus' divinity must not be allowed to obscure his humanity.
Exactly the same principle comes into play in the case of the sacraments. Whatever else a sacramental ritual is, it is a human action, a
human experience, a human expression which originates from man.
This by no means precludes a connection with the numinous, with
the presence of God in the world of man. Still, christian faith
remains a faith that finds a transcendent God in finite experience;
and history shows clearly enough that christianity obscures its own
most basic insight when it starts reaching into the world of magical
understanding. If we are to interpret the ritual of the eucharist accurately, we need a sacramental language that will take seriously the
humanness of the action and the finiteness of the people and objects
involved in it.

2

Two Questions About Reality

Most of our sacramental language is distinctly sacred language. It begins with God or the sacraments given by God, and it ends with man. One of the first things a child learns from his catechism is that "God gave us the sacraments." Baptism makes us members of Christ's body; in the eucharist the Lord feeds his people; in the sacrament of penance the sinner is reconciled with God through the church; and so on. One first learns what the sacraments are for, what they do, what God does through them. Perhaps this is the only starting point that can be taken in a catechetical situation. But this approach can backfire after one has been exposed to it over a long period of years. It can give the impression that the sacraments finally belong more to God than to ourselves. Our ordinary religious language "divinizes" the sacraments without taking account of their origin from within man's experience.

Anyone who possesses an adult faith has gone through some kind of process of questioning the system with which he grew up: a church, a way to God, a way to live, and an organized set of rituals for every occasion. Frequently, though, the questioning process can get nowhere because one is left with nothing but a sacred language which makes sense only within the very system which is being questioned. This gives us the curious phenomenon of people who become upset or even throw the whole thing overboard when they discover that ideas like virgin birth or the resurrection of a god-man existed long before Jesus, or that the sacraments are all rooted in primitive pagan rituals. I call the phenomenon curious, because the very thing that anchors christian theology and ritual to humanity and the experience of mankind should be anything but an argument against faith. This is what I mean by saying that much of our religious language eventually backfires. Sacred language easily becomes meaningless language, and preaching or catechetics which possesses nothing more than sacred language is destined to provoke unnecessary crises of faith.

This touches on one of the most important insights of Vatican II, which realized that the church could no longer see itself simply from within or attempt to define itself as if from inside an enclosed shell. The church is not the center of everything; it points *to* the center. It is a body of people who are conscious that in Jesus something decisive has happened to the world. The church aims at being in the world as a light on the mountain top, yeast in the dough, a seed planted in the earth. These are images not of what the church actually is, but of what it strives to be, with all of the imperfection and failure it shares with the rest of mankind. And if we talk about ourselves as the body of Christ, the people of God, or whatever, none of this sacred language means anything except *in relation to* the world. The church cannot understand its own efforts to be a living embodiment of Jesus' love and freedom and peace except in relation to the world's own best efforts toward freedom and unity and peace. The church tries explicitly to become what the world implicitly is looking for. A good many sections of the documents of Vatican II struggle with this relationship between the church and the world, showing new respect for the world and for man's efforts toward humanization of the world.[1]

Just as the church loses its true identity if it is cut off from the world, so the sacramental signs with which we worship lose their human meaning if they are defined strictly from within the sacramental system. Ideas like "God feeds his people in the eucharist" or "Christ is present in the eucharist" have a meaning, but the meaning can easily be lost. The things we say about light bulbs or dishwashers rarely become unreal; good light bulbs and dishwashers have to do with the correct functioning of cold empirical realities like filaments, timers and mechanisms. Our sacred language, on the other hand, which reaches beyond the realm of the empirical, does not contain built-in controls which demand realism in what we say. Sacred language can snowball, expressing not only man's search for God but also his desire for some magical power to come along and subdue the nastiness of the finite. Sacred language often wants burnt-out light bulbs and broken-down dishwashers to work. In its search for the transcendent it can break loose from the empirical. This is why the church has at times defined itself as something which it is not. It is also why the eucharistic bread and wine have sometimes become something which they are not. "Christ is present in the eucharist" can make sense. But it will make sense only if we can locate expressions like this in a world which also speaks of light bulbs and dishwashers.

There are basically two ways we go about interpreting finite reality, two questions we ask about our experience of the finite. By "finite reality" I simply mean the things we run into, the events and people and happenings and objects that impinge upon us. Implicitly or explicitly, we react to these things and experiences in two ways. Implicitly or explicitly, we ask two sorts of questions of the things that happen around us and to us. The questions can be schematized this way:

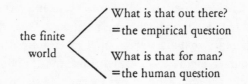

the finite world

What is that out there?
= the empirical question

What is that for man?
= the human question

The first question is the factual question. That is a truck thunder-ing down upon me at a speed of some fifty miles an hour, and unless I get out of the way I am going to be hurt. It makes no difference whether it is a Mack truck or a GMC truck, and my dog will react the same way I do. The second question is irrelevant at this point; the truck in this situation has no *human* meaning. With my human intelligence I could calculate the weight and acceleration of the truck, the relative harm its velocity could do, and the relative merits of one make of truck over another. I can always ask those questions and give an erudite human answer. But I have not yet asked *man's* question. Despite my ability to measure the speed and velocity of the truck, both I and my dog are going to react to the event in exactly the same way, by getting out of the road.

The first question, the first level of perceiving events, has to do with the interpretation of signals. Smoke signals fire, wet streets in-dicate rain, and a rapidly moving truck signals destruction for any-thing that gets in its way. I know this from my experience, and Fido knows it from his. The fact that I can abstract from my experience and formulate rules about cause and effect does not change the na-ture of the experience, where I react without having to reason. Trucks that move and light bulbs that burn and dishwashers that work affect a great deal of our behavior and occupy much of our mental time. This is nothing demeaning. But at this level of percep-tion one has not yet asked the question of *human* meaning.

At the second level of questioning, where man deals with man, it can matter whether one's truck is a GMC or a Mack. If I own a car that doesn't start on extremely cold mornings, I share an empirical fact with many of my neighbors. But if my car happens to be a Continental or a Cadillac, the fact that it won't start is a fact I might not be too interested in sharing with my neighbors. Certainly it would make no difference to Fido, who would make little distinction between one running engine and another. Like myself, Fido appreciates that the sun gives heat and light; but for me, the sun is also warmth and brightness. It symbolizes something, it says something more than its physical self. This of course does not change the physical self of the sun or the Cadillac. What they say to man (the second question) is all tied up with what they are (the first question). It is because the sun gives light and heat that it can *mean* warmth and brightness; and the Cadillac is a status symbol precisely because of the physical properties and equipment it is endowed with.

This is not simply a matter of the "objective" and the "subjective," though the latter is a rather commonly accepted distinction. It usually implies that whenever we talk about light bulbs or dishwashers or the sun rising in the morning, we are talking about the objective order; on the other hand, whenever we say anything about human values or symbols or religion, we are dealing with the subjective. Wherever this distinction operates, we usually find an enshrinement of the empirical question, the first question; the second question becomes subordinate to the first because it is "not objective." When people say "That's *only* a symbol," they are implying that the second question does not bring us as closely in touch with reality as the first, and thus that the symbolic and the real are somehow opposed. This whole attitude (which revolves implicitly around the objective-subjective distinction) has taken its toll in theology, especially sacramental theology, because it has made us mistrust the category of the symbolic. This is why many christians are deeply disturbed when they hear the eucharistic presence frankly described as a symbolic presence; for whatever else "symbolic" may mean to them, it certainly means "not real."

Part of the confusion can be straightened out simply by noting that both the first and the second questions are at once objective and subjective. The empirical question is objective inasmuch as it asks for hard facts, a description of what that is out there, or what actually happened out there. But the question also has its subjective aspect because it involves our mental perception of what that is out there. An animal reacts to a sunrise or to a rapidly moving truck according to patterns of cause and effect he has learned from his experience; man behaves according to much the same patterns, and of course he can go on to formulate laws of cause and effect based on his experience. But in either case, at the empirical level of behavior or questioning, we are dealing with perception and therefore with one form of subjectivity.

As for the second level of questioning, the human question, no one would deny its subjective aspect. But that second question is also an *objective* question because the answer we give to it does not leave us locked up in pure subjectivity. If the sun symbolizes warmth and brightness in the human sense of those terms, it does so because it gives heat and light; and the human meaning of the sun is *objectively* different from the human meaning of a grey and cloudy day. This is true not just for myself but for millions of people. Of course, we all have symbols that are personal to ourselves alone. "What is that for man?" can often mean "What is that for me alone?" Only I can know the human meaning of, let us say, a book given to me by a close friend on a special occasion in my life. But the fact that this is a *personal* meaning does not make it any less *objective*. My answer to the human question here is rooted in the empirical fact that a friend gave me a gift.

The two questions are therefore two different ways of getting at reality. They are complementary ways of sinking one's teeth into reality, and insofar as they are both ways of *interpreting* reality, they both have their subjective and objective aspects. Susanne Langer uses an excellent image to express this interlocking: the factual and the symbolic make up the *warp and woof of the fabric of meaning*.[2] The interweaving is of course complex. The color green elicits a simple response at the empirical level when it appears in a traffic light; exactly the same color has human and symbolic meanings when it appears in a painting or a poem.

The difficulty is that the fabric can and does break down. This is seen in the tendency to view the empirical question as the only question which really puts us in touch with "objective reality." The technological society and the age of space exploration have come about as a result of a perfectly valid interest in the first question. But this development, as we hear and read constantly these days, has raised fantastic human problems because we have systematically neglected the human question. When a society finds its most significant values in how much a person earns or how fast one can get from one place to another, the second question is swallowed up in the first, and progress *becomes* human meaning.

Opting for material values as the most important human values is of course not a new phenomenon. People of every era have been drawn in this direction, whether wealth lay within their reach or not. Fairy tales about princes and beautiful ladies and happy endings in splendid palaces were undoubtedly first told in peasant cottages, not in the royal banquet hall. The problem for us is that technical progress and the wealth it promises have been the *main* preoccupation of the era. Construction of freeways and rapid movement from one town to another in ever larger automobiles and airplanes seem to be good things—until one starts trying to pin down the exact human "good" of speed and mobility. A higher standard of living is sought by everyone, but no one is quite sure just what "higher" means. What it means in most cases is quite simple: the empirical question tends simply to *become* the human question.

The human worth of simple everyday activities is a problem for the man or woman of the late twentieth century. Hard work, parenthood, and civic life once had definite values which were simplistically but clearly enough symbolized in the american dream of prosperity, the flag, motherhood and apple pie. Twentieth-century americans

have had these values drummed into them, and advertising constantly evokes them; but one wonders to what extent they are factual
twentieth-century realities.

Most men never see the goods they produce, but stand by a traveling belt
and turn a million identical passing screws or close a million identical passing wrappers in a succession of hours, days, years. This sort of activity is too
poor, too empty, for even the most ingenious mind to invest it with symbolic content. Work is no longer a sphere of ritual; and so the nearest and
surest source of mental satisfaction has dried up.[3]

Mrs. Langer wrote these words shortly before World War II, when
the american dream still said much more to people than it says now,
and long before the counterculture of the late 1960's brought the
tyranny of technology and its implicit values to national attention. If
anything, the human problem has become more severe. The white-
collar workers and computer technologists of our decade are still further removed from the product that is made and sold. Still fewer
people know the carpenter and plumber who helped build the dwell-
ing they live in.

Work has become monotonous to the point where the fatigue factor interferes with productivity. The success of Muzak in offices and
factories stems from the idea that productivity might be increased if
the monotony of work is relieved by music. But what kind of music?
Artistic, creative music? No, such music would attract attention to itself. What is needed is functional music—music chosen, as one writer puts it, on the principle that "boring work is made less boring by
boring music."[4] In a cultural atmosphere where human progress is
implicitly identified with technical progress, it is only natural that an
art form like music should be banalized and put at the service of productivity. In just the same way, the highest forms of human expression can be reduced to depersonalized technique. The famous Mas-
ters and Johnson study, *Human Sexual Response,* gives a detailed

account of changes in body chemistry during coitus. Couples are hooked up to a barrage of instruments and data is collected. Whatever merits the study has on its own, it is symptomatic of the wider cultural tendency to reduce what can be the most intimate of human experiences to an impersonal physiological encounter, in which how well you perform is more important than whom you are with or what the action is saying.

We are not yet fully aware of the extent to which we have enshrined the empirical level of looking at things. A man who raises value questions when he is at home with his wife and family might not be in a position to do much about such questions at work, if indeed the questions even occur to him there. Some years ago, a large american corporation which owned a banana plantation in Central America decided that a particular shipload of bananas, if put on the market, would upset the market and jeopardize the company's investments. The bananas were dumped into the sea. The banana pickers, who had been paid well above the average wage of other laborers in their country, protested violently. When told about this protest some time later, an american businessman was perplexed. "But why should they get so excited? They were generously paid for their work."

It is not difficult to find other examples of cases where we reduce human meaning to economic and technological progress. The movement for women's liberation, for instance, asks questions about the value of woman, her image as mother and sex partner, her freedom, her role in society. These are valid second-level questions, and extremely pressing ones. But it is interesting that some of the heroines of the movement are women who have decided that real freedom is to be found in successfully entering that world where technical progress is seen as human progress. There is no reason to insist that a woman must find her personhood in being a mother and a baker of apple pies. Religious women have known this for many long centuries, and most married women have undoubtedly been much more than their husbands ever thought they were. The problem in our day seems to be whether the male world, so dedicated to the empirical question and to economic and technological manipulation of "what that is out there," is going to impose its definition of priorities on women's quest for freedom and womanhood.

It is hard for us to project ourselves back into an age when the empirical question was not the first nor the more important question for people. There was a time when the world out there, the world of nature, was a very integral part of man's own awareness of himself. Take the moon. Most readers will remember the time before one could ask the question "What can we use the moon for?" The song "Shine on, harvest moon, for me and my gal" is out of date for more than musical reasons; it evokes a symbolic attitude toward the moon which becomes quite difficult to sustain once the moon becomes just another body to be explored. But even so relatively recent a song still contains echoes of the way man *first* perceived the moon. It was intimately related to his own life. It was a mysterious orb which affected the rhythm of nature, fertility, the powers of life, love itself. It was a god or goddess in its own right, so powerful was its influence.

The same thing applied to simple realities like earth and water. Today few people are close enough to the land to know it as Mother Earth. But that is how the land was first perceived. It was not a neutral substance but a power, one which could be called "mother" because it possessed all the mysterious forces and influences of a mother. It is no accident that the ancient creation story found in the Book of Genesis spoke of man's being formed out of the clay of the earth (Gen 2:7). The connection here is really untranslatable; *adam* (man) is made from *adamah* (earth), so that in this story man is by definition "earth-being." The process of emerging from the womb and becoming physically and psychically independent of the womb is a lengthy process for any person. In just the same way, it took a long time before man could even *define* himself apart from the earth, which symbolized all that a mother is.

As for water, this commodity has been so bottled up and brought under man's control that it takes a disaster like drought or a flood to reawaken in us what primitive man felt so deeply. For him, water was a life-bearing force so basic to human existence that it symbolized life, it "spoke" life, the origin of life, the womb itself. In Genesis, the creation of life begins with God's mastery over the watery abyss (Gen 1:2). But water is also a death-dealing force, and so it appears as God's agent of destruction in the days of Noah. Because it speaks both life and death, ancient man perceived water as a mediator between the two. This idea is embodied in the story of the hebrews' passage through the waters of the Red Sea, a passage from death to life.

Christian baptism of course makes use of all this symbolism, and the new roman rite for baptism sharpens and highlights the ancient ideas. The difficulty for us is that when baptism is explained, we are not usually satisfied until we *translate* the water symbolism into some other language. The person baptized "becomes a member of the community of faith" and he is "made to share the fruits of Christ's redemptive work." Such statements are true, but they are also colorless. Compare most any recent sermon on baptism with this explanation given by Cyril of Jerusalem in the fourth century:

After the anointing you were conducted by the hand to the holy pool of sacred baptism, just as Christ was conveyed from the cross to the sepulchre close at hand. Each person was asked if he believed in the name of the Father and of the Son and of the Holy Spirit. You made the confession that brings salvation, and submerged yourselves three times in the water and emerged: by this symbolic gesture you were secretly re-enacting the burial of Christ three days in the tomb. . . . In one and the same action you died and were born; the water of salvation became both tomb and mother for you. What Solomon said of others is apposite to you. On that occasion he said: "There is a time to be born, and a time to die." But the opposite is true in your case—there is a time to die and a time to be born. A single moment achieves both ends, and your begetting was simultaneous with your death.[5]

"The water became both *tomb and mother* for you." When the church fathers explained baptism, they appealed not to abstractions but to radical experiences of what water is *for man,* what water *means* to man in his innermost psyche. The basic symbolism was expanded through the notion of "figures" and their "fulfillment." Christian baptism is "prefigured" by the great flood, by the crossing of the Red Sea, by the healing of Naaman the Syrian who was cured of leprosy when he washed in the Jordan. All these figures were "fulfilled" in the death and resurrection of Jesus, which we symbolically re-enact in the ritual of baptism. But the language of figure and fulfillment makes human sense only because man first saw water as a radical symbol of life and death. It is to this experience, this perception, that early christian catechesis appealed. Of course, the baptismal rite itself was much richer in those days: one was actually immersed in the water, indeed three times (the basic baptismal action was expanded to express faith in the trinity and Christ's three days in the tomb). But if later christian practice reduced baptism to the act of pouring a few drops of water over the forehead, it was because the archetypal meaning of water became virtually forgotten.

Depth psychology reminds us that archetypal symbols like earth and water still operate in our unconscious and manifest themselves, for instance, in our dreams. But the old symbols have little hold on our everyday *conscious* behavior. In this sense, we are different people from those to whom Cyril of Jerusalem explained the "heavenly mystery of baptism." How did we get where we are, where it is so difficult to recover the basic meanings man once saw in the world around him? The answer to this question has to do with the evolution of thought, particularly as it took place in the western world.

The evolution is a fascinating one, and the strange science of alchemy holds an important place in it. Alchemy seems to have originated in the mediterranean world during the first centuries of the christian era. Alchemists wanted to make gold from base materials like lead—a venture which sounds to us like a hopelessly naive attempt at some sort of magic. But much more is going on here than meets the eye. The alchemical process consisted of various stages, beginning with base matter (represented by the color black), then quicksilver (white), then sulphur (red), and finally gold. Why this process, and why was it expected to work? Because this is the way *man* works. In our own interior world, we begin with the soul in its original condition, a condition of darkness and guilt (black). We go through initial transformation (white) and the purification that comes through passion, suffering, conflict (red). And we are finally destined for salvation, perfection, wholeness, all that comes from a union of the preceding opposites (gold). The alchemical principle was *Solve et coagula:* "Analyse all the elements in yourself, dissolve all that is inferior in you, even though you may break in doing so; then, with the strength acquired from the preceding operation, congeal."[6]

The gold for which many alchemists searched was therefore not ordinary gold. For many, the symbolism took over the material reality of the symbol. "You will never make Oneness out of Otherness until you yourself have become Oneness." What the alchemists did was to project man's *interior* process of psychic growth onto the *exterior* world of inanimate matter. They assumed that the question "What is that out there, and how do I manipulate it?" could be answered by working according to the model of interior growth which mankind had laboriously learned over the ages. In short, they thought empirical questions could be answered with principles coming from second-level questions. And why shouldn't this work? If *man* has to go through various transformations in order to become what he should be—whole, free, gold—why shouldn't the same rules apply to matter?

The projection didn't work, of course. As the centuries passed, it became clear that the material world did not operate according to quite the same rules as those of the psychic world. And if man had learned something about his own inner development, he had not yet learned the empirical "laws" that govern the workings of the material universe. Those laws were gradually uncovered as experimental scientific methods were developed, tested, re-tested. The process was long and slow. But by the seventeenth century, discoveries of the laws of nature began coming rapidly, one on the heels of another.

A curious shift then took place, as western man became more and more intrigued with his discoveries and excited with their possibilities. He began to construct systems in which the new and successful *empirical* theories became the model for *every* kind of understanding, including the understanding of God. Leibniz (+1716) was able to describe God as the perfect geometrician, the perfect orderer of the universe. "It can be said that God as architect satisfies God as lawgiver in everything, and that sins must therefore carry their punishment with them *by the order of nature,* and even *by virtue of the mechanical structure of things.*"[7] Empirical understanding was thus becoming the model for understanding religious ideas. In this atmosphere miracles, which once meant signs of God's presence among men, came to have a scientific meaning which would have been quite inconceivable to the biblical authors who wrote about miracles. In this late scientific age, miracles came to mean interruptions in nature, divine exceptions to empirical laws. Voltaire (+1778) was perfectly logical in rejecting miracles on these grounds. In his treatise *Of Miracles,* he argued very soundly that God either foresaw the necessity for a exception to his immutable laws, or he did not foresee it. If he foresaw it, he must have made the necessary regulations of the law in the beginning; if he did not foresee it, he is no longer God.

Here were the thought models inherited by the nineteenth and twentieth centuries. The drive to manipulate matter led to the discovery of empirical principles, which then became the primary model for interpreting practically everything else. In our century, psychology and the sciences of human behavior have had to shake themselves free of faulty presuppositions coming from physical science—or rather, from a use of the methods of physical science where those methods do not apply. Theology is no exception here. Much damage has been done, and much atheism generated, by conceiving of God as a super-orderer who operates according to the same rules as does the physical universe. This God is worlds removed from the God who is love, the Father of Jesus Christ, who in entirely too recent times had to bend to the inexorable Executor of the laws of the universe.

We look on alchemy as a foolish endeavor. How silly to think that material phenomena can be explained by models drawn from inner experience or from second-level questioning! But the flip-side of the coin is no different. Is it any less foolish to think that man's interior human growth can be fully explained by the laws of matter? Behavioral psychology has not yet really come to terms with this question, and the theories of a behaviorist like B. F. Skinner have to be subjected to the same basic methodological question that we ask of the alchemists. If the alchemists went astray in projecting the model of psychic evolution onto matter, to what extent can the laws of matter provide a model for understanding inner psychic growth?

***

These pages have attacked a good many elements in the concept of technological progress. I must admit that there is a strange and perhaps hypocritical element in the attack. The words on this page are the product of ink and paper mills, a typewriter and a printing press, not to mention basics like electricity and light bulbs. Plato, Jesus, and Johann Sebastian Bach would have been astounded at such "basics." Our problem is that all these things are useful, so useful that they become valuable, so valuable that they start controlling values, and controlling them to such an extent that manipulation of material reality becomes the *really* real. Every thinking person knows this is not so. But we do not always think, because our very freedom to *ask* the human question is jeopardized by preoccupation with the empirical question.

Perhaps this is why Saint-Exupéry's fable, *The Little Prince*, has become a modern classic. The whole story makes a plea for imagination, for fantasy. It keeps driving away at the point that "what is essential is invisible to the eye." In making this point the story insists, from the first page to the last, that contemporary man must rediscover our second question, the question he seems most reluctant to ask. At one point the narrator and the little prince, walking through the desert, come upon a well. Both are thirsty, and the narrator draws up a bucket of water for them to drink. The narrator sees this as a simple event, something to be interpreted in a straightforward factual sort of way, until the little prince forces him to ask the human question.

"I am thirsty for this water," said the little prince. "Give me some of it to drink . . ."

And I understood what he had been looking for.

I raised the bucket to his lips. He drank, his eyes closed. It was as sweet as some special festival treat. This water was indeed a different thing from ordinary nourishment. Its sweetness was born of the walk under the stars, the song of the pulley, the effort of my arms. It was good for the heart, like a present. When I was a little boy, the lights of the Christmas tree, the music of the Midnight Mass, the tenderness of smiling faces, used to make up, so, the radiance of the gifts I received.

"The men where you live," said the little prince, "raise five thousand roses in the same garden—and they do not find in it what they are looking for."

"And yet what they are looking for could be found in one single rose, or in a little water."

"Yes, that is true," I said.

And the little prince added:

"But the eyes are blind. One must look with the heart . . ."[8]

Those last words and a good many of the earlier ones can easily be turned into sentimental slogans. The human question can be turned into a purely emotional question, and "seeing with the heart" can be reduced to a matter of warm feelings and good vibes. According to innumerable books and movies and popular songs, seeing with the heart means turning on to another person—and turning off to most of the rest of reality. Search for human value and for what is invisible to the eye can become a form of escapism as immature and limited as its opposite extreme of preoccupation with the empirical, the merely visible.

The Little Prince rises above sentimentality by asking not how we are to *feel* about reality but how we are to *see* it. Saint-Exupéry is concerned above all with *perception*. A single rose or a little water can contain the really real only if one's fabric of meaning is a whole fabric. What is most humanly real about them can be grasped only if one's perceptions are whole, and yet there is no question of turning the rose or the water into something they are not.

The passage just quoted makes essentially the same point as the conclusion of John's gospel. "Happy are those who have not seen and yet have believed" (Jn 20:29). The point here is that the believer is the one who *really* sees. John of course is talking about faith, and there are a great many things that need to be said about the perception of reality which we call "faith." But basically, faith is one form of second-level perception, a form of seeing things that answers to the question "What is that for man?" And so a faith-view of reality and human experience presupposes that one knows how to perceive reality in the manner of the little prince.

If the human or symbolic question is the woof of the fabric of meaning, the empirical or factual question is its warp. And if the fabric breaks down with neglect of the human question, it will also be undone if it loses its warp. The single rose and the little bit of water can always be made into something other than what they are. In the last chapter we saw examples of what happens, both to Jesus and to christian worship, when the factual question is not asked along with the symbolic question. Alchemy, too, failed because it could not adequately distinguish the two questions. So we have to face the fact that the old symbols have often exercised unrealistic controls over people's lives.

Our religious symbolism today—where it is not entirely lost—is much less ornate than that of an earlier age, when every conceivable area of life had a religious value attached to it, a religious symbol to interpret it, and a ritual or prayer to control it. If esteem for the empirical has led many people to reject religion, it has also made religion look into its symbolism and purify it. But anyone who has made religion a part of his or her life will admit that there are people whose lives are still deeply affected by symbols which have gotten out of hand. One need only think of the symbolism connected with sin and its forgiveness, God and the devil, confession and repentance, heaven and hell. While such symbols provide a genuine means of understanding and coping with evil and guilt, there is no doubt that for many people christian symbolism has also fostered guilt.

Preoccupation with technical progress, then, is not the only thing that jeopardizes our freedom of mind. Religious symbols, meant to interpret human life and free the human spirit, have also been known to enslave it. Our challenge is to hold the factual and symbolic questions together, keep the fabric of meaning from unraveling, and enable christians to interpret their experience in a way that will produce something whole.

The Last Supper and the Eucharist

THE TWO questions about reality have to be asked about the christian eucharist. If this is to be done with any accuracy, and if our assertions about the eucharist are to remain anchored to reality and to the real Jesus, we should begin by looking at the last supper. Asked of a past event, the two questions take on an historical character. The empirical or factual question has to do with what actually happened; the symbolic question deals with the human and religious meaning of what happened.

the last supper
- What did Jesus and his disciples do?
- What was the meaning of what they did?

The second question has to be handled in various stages: What did the action mean to the people there present? What did it mean to the New Testament writers? What did it mean to a later era? Distinguishing these stages is important if we are to sort out different layers of interpretation, or check later interpretations against the earliest ones.

The first question is rather easily handled, at least so far as the basics are concerned. What Jesus and his friends did was to have a meal together, a meal which had ritual connotations. In our day political organizations, sections of industry, societies for the promotion of ecology, or bowling teams will get together for dinner at a Holiday Inn to commemorate or celebrate a particular occasion, or to provide the proper human setting for a business meeting. The situation was not that much different in Jesus' day. We tend to look upon the jewish religion of his time as a huge institutional church, unified in its religious views and goals and ultimately united against Jesus of Nazareth and his disciples. But the large institutional churches of our day had no real parallel in Jesus' time; his contemporaries experienced the same sort of division and sectarianism that we do today. The gospels allude to this when they bring up the conflict of opinion between the pharisees and the sadducees over the question of the resurrection of the dead. But even apart from doctrinal disagreements, there were within the jewish congregations of that time small informal groups of friends who gathered because of a particular religious interest. These groups, among which Jesus' group would have been numbered, had meals together, even weekly, when they would meet for fellowship and conversation as well as to take care of their business.

Every jewish meal is a ritual meal, and the suppers held by these small societies of friends would have been no different, except that the ritual customs were probably observed with somewhat more formality than at an ordinary family meal. No dish was eaten without a prayer of thanksgiving or blessing, a *berakah*, which the host or the leader of the group said over each kind of food as it was served. Near the beginning of the meal, for example, the host took bread and broke it, saying "Blessed are you, Lord our God, eternal king, for bringing forth bread from the earth." He then gave a piece of the bread to everyone at the table. The main course followed with similar blessings for each dish. If wine was served, each person would bless his own cup every time he refilled it, saying "Blessed are you, Lord our God, eternal king, for making the fruit of the vine." At the end of the meal, especially on more solemn occasions, came a longer prayer of thanksgiving.

Leader: Let us give thanks.
All assembled: Blessed be the name of the Lord from this time forth and forever.
Leader: Let us bless our God of whose bounty we have partaken.
All assembled: Blessed be our God of whose bounty we have partaken and through whose goodness we live.
Leader: Blessed are you, Lord our God, king of the universe. You feed the whole world with your goodness, with grace, with loving kindness and tender mercy. You give food to all flesh, for your loving kindness endures forever. Through your great goodness food has never failed us. May it not fail us forever and ever, for your great name's sake; for you nourish and sustain all beings, and do good to all, and you provide food for all your creatures. Blessed are you Lord, for giving food to all.

We thank you, Lord our God, for giving as a heritage to our fathers a desirable, good and ample land, and for bringing us forth from the land of Egypt and delivering us from the house of bondage. We thank you for your covenant which you have sealed in our flesh, your Torah which you have taught us, your statutes which you have made known to us, the life and grace and loving kindness which you have bestowed upon us. . . .

Have mercy, Lord our God, on Israel your people, on Jerusalem your city, on Zion the abiding place of your glory, on the kingdom of the house of David your anointed, and on the great and holy house that was called by your name. Our God, our Father, feed us, nourish us, sustain, support, and relieve us. And speedily, Lord our God, grant us relief from all our troubles. . . .

May we receive a blessing from the Lord, and righteousness from the

God of our salvation. And may we find grace and good understanding in the sight of God and man.[1]

Christian eucharistic prayers have their own complex history, but it is not difficult to see their origins in a prayer like this one. The idea behind the earlier, shorter blessings has been brought back into the roman liturgy in the prayers recited at the preparation of the gifts. On a more solemn occasion the long concluding prayer of thanksgiving, known simply as "the blessing," was recited over a special cup of wine, which was then passed around to everyone at table when the prayer was finished. This is undoubtedly the ritual custom Paul refers to when he talks about "the cup of blessing which we bless" (1 Cor 10:16).

Here, very briefly and stripped of details, are the ritual customs that were associated with family meals or fellowship meals in Jesus' time. Variations were made depending on the occasion or the particular religious emphasis of the group. The passover meal itself, seen against this background, is simply an annual meal with special foods and blessings. But whatever the variations, the basic ritual character of the jewish meal comes into play: prayers of blessing recited over each kind of food, and a concluding prayer of thanksgiving often recited over a cup of wine.

This is the starting point for answering our second question, regarding what Jesus and his friends understood by what they did at the last supper. Even apart from any association with the passover feast, their meal already had a symbolic value; it was already a ritual meal. Whatever we mean by saying that Jesus "instituted the eucharist," it cannot mean that he instituted a new ritual. Every christian is familiar with the New Testament accounts of the last supper and Jesus' command to "do this in memory of me." But we get the whole thing backwards if we understand this command as meaning that we are to remember Jesus by doing something new and unusual. We are of course affected by our culture; for us it *is* unusual to break bread or share a cup with accompanying prayers anywhere but in church. But whatever the command to "do this" may have meant, it was not a command to break bread or share the cup.

Gregory Dix handles this point very effectively in his classic work *The Shape of the Liturgy*. To break bread and give thanks, in just the way Jesus did, was an obligation for every devout jew. Jesus was neither instituting a new ritual nor telling his friends to continue an existing ritual: it would be pointless to command something that would go on in any case. The real meaning therefore falls on the last half of the command. Do this *in memory of me*. That is, whenever you do this in the future, whenever you gather for a meal and do what we have so often done together, you will be remembering *me* in what you do. What Jesus did, then, was to attach a new meaning to the most ordinary ritual in jewish life—indeed, to the only ritual or corporate act he could be sure his disciples would do together regularly in any case.[2]

It is difficult to determine historically what sort of meal the last supper was. Was it the passover meal itself? Was it an ordinary fellowship meal of the sort I have been describing (which of course would have had a special significance because of Jesus' impending arrest)? Scholars argue the point. Mark, Matthew and Luke present it as a passover meal. But in that case Jesus and his friends anticipated the official celebration; John makes this point, noting that when the jews brought Jesus to Pilate they had not yet eaten the passover (Jn 18:28). John's own treatment of the last supper is consistent with this remark, for he does not call it a passover meal.

There have been many attempts to reconcile this conflict between John and the synoptic authors. The answers have ranged from the simplistic (Christ is God, and he could celebrate the passover whenever he liked) to the scholarly. An attempt has been made, for instance, to show that two different liturgical calendars were followed by the jews of that time. According to this hypothesis Jesus and his disciples, in celebrating the passover early, were following an older calendar which was just as acceptable as the "official" calendar to which John refers. This is Annie Jaubert's thesis, and she argues it on the grounds that we must not compromise "the historical character of the very clear statement of the synoptics."[3] But there is no reason to assume that the primary intent of these writers in this instance is historical rather than theological. One of the earliest faith-understandings of Jesus is that he is the new passover; Paul mentions this in one of the earliest New Testament writings (1 Cor 5:7). The theme of Christ "our passover who has been sacrificed" would easily have become associated with the event of the last supper because of its proximity to the hebrew passover and of course to Jesus' own sacrificial death. Thus the idea that the last supper was a passover meal could be a *theological interpretation* on the part of the synoptic writers rather than an *historical statement*. Or to put it in terms of our two questions, this would not be the first time the gospel writers were answering the symbolic question rather than the purely factual one.

In any case, that last meal with Jesus could not have been completely tied up with the passover meal in the religious consciousness of the disciples. If this were so, it would be hard to see how they would have followed the command to "do this in memory of me" more than once a year. The thought of celebrating the passover any oftener than that simply could not have occurred to any good jew. Yet we know from various remarks and stories in the New Testament that the first christians met regularly for the breaking of the bread. The symbolism of the jewish ritual meal—*any* ritual meal—therefore underlies whatever other symbolism may have been in play at the last supper. Jesus gave a new meaning not just to the passover meal but to any meal for which his friends would gather in the future.

But why bread and wine? Why should these two elements have been singled out from among the many other dishes that would have been served at that important meal?

Here again Jesus was not an innovator. During the past few decades, especially since the discovery of the famous Dead Sea scrolls, we have learned much about the religious practices of various monastic communities that existed in the wilderness of Palestine before and during Jesus' time. The documents we now possess are a sharp reminder that there were many more ideas abroad in the judaism of that era than one might gather from a casual reading of the gospels, which concentrate heavily on the judaism of the pharisees. Qumran is probably the best known of these desert communities, but there were others as well. John the Baptist undoubtedly came from one of them, and scholars debate whether Jesus himself might have had some personal contact with the wilderness groups, particularly during his earlier years. In any case, there is little doubt that their main ideas and religious practices would have been known to Jesus and his followers.

One important practice of the Qumran sect was a ritual meal presided over by a priest who, at the beginning of the meal, pronounced a blessing over the first-fruits of bread and wine. These meals looked forward to a messianic banquet when the two messiahs would be present: a priest-messiah, a descendant of Aaron; and a king-messiah, the messiah of Israel. There were even rules laid down for how that ideal banquet was to be celebrated in the age to come.

When they gather for the community table, or to drink wine, and arrange the community table and mix the wine to drink, let no man stretch out his hand over the first-fruits of bread and wine before the priest [the priest-messiah]. For it is he who shall bless the first-fruits of bread and wine, and shall first stretch out his hand over the bread. And afterwards, the messiah of Israel [the king-messiah] shall stretch out his hands over the bread. And afterwards, all the congregation of the community shall bless, each according to his rank. And they shall proceed according to this rite at every meal where at least ten persons are assembled.[4]

This was the liturgy of the age to come, the messianic liturgy, and it was anticipated at the daily supper held in every community where at least ten members were present. The note of anticipation is significant. The gospels sound the same note when they report the last supper—as in Mark, where Jesus tells his disciples that he "will never again drink of the fruit of the vine until the day when I drink it new in the kingdom of God" (Mk 14:25). The first christians clearly understood their eucharistic meals in connection with the ideal age to come. This is echoed in Paul's insistence that "every time you eat this bread and drink this cup, you proclaim the death of the Lord *until he comes*" (1 Cor 11:26).

Such eucharistic themes become all the more intelligible against the background of the Qumran supper ritual. As I emphasized earlier, the last supper makes no sense apart from Jesus' own awareness that he was indeed the messiah (however any of his contemporaries may have understood that idea)—his awareness that his impending death was to have a profound and central religious significance for the coming reign of God which he had been preaching. It seems that at the last supper the disciples had not yet caught on to what Jesus himself understood by messiahship. But if they knew anything of the Qumran practice, Jesus' action at the meal would at least have been recognizable to them as an action with messianic implications. They would have had no trouble understanding that their last meal with the master had become a ritual meal with a new religious significance. Their problem was how to understand that in this man Jesus the messianic age had really come, and this understanding broke in on them only with the easter experience.

Whatever influence the Qumran practice may have had on the actual form of the last supper, it seems to have influenced some of the earliest christian communities. In a document called *The Didache* or *The Teaching of the Apostles*—which may be as old as a number of the New Testament writings—we find these instructions for blessing bread and wine at the beginning of the meal:

Give thanks in this way. First, over the cup: "We give thanks to you, our Father, for the holy vine of your son David, which you have made known to us through Jesus your son. To you be glory forever." Then over the broken bread: "We give thanks to you, our Father, for the life and knowledge you have made known to us through Jesus your son. To you be glory forever. As this broken bread was once scattered grain on the hillsides and was gathered together and made one, so let your church be gathered together from the ends of the earth into your kingdom. For yours is the glory and the power through Jesus Christ forever and ever."[5]

This text echoes the Qumran practice and dovetails with Mark's and Matthew's accounts of the last supper, which suggest that Jesus blessed the *bread and wine together* at the *beginning* of the meal (Mk 14:22; Mt 26:26). Paul and Luke, on the other hand, speak of his blessing the *bread at the beginning* and the *cup at the end* of the meal (Lk 22:20; 1 Cor 11:25). This latter, as we saw earlier, was the common jewish custom.

When we lay the six texts side by side—the Qumran *Rule*, the *Didache*, and the last supper narratives in Mark, Matthew, Luke and Paul—we are reminded of several points. First, the accounts of the last supper found in the New Testament are influenced by the actual eucharistic practices of the particular christian communities in which they were written. Just as there were variations in jewish rituals for meals, so there were differences in the way the first christians celebrated their eucharists. Secondly, whatever connection the first christians made between the last supper and the passover meal, a far more basic factor at work in their minds was the religious significance of a corporate meal. And in the context of such a meal, the elements of bread and wine already had a special significance, indeed a messianic one, long before the last supper.

It should be mentioned that there are many counts on which Jesus' teachings disagree sharply with that of the wilderness sectarians. The daily life of these monks was filled with one prescribed washing after another (someone has remarked that it seems they never got out of the bathtub). They had a detailed code of laws with strict penalties for violations, even accidental failures: man was definitely made for the sabbath. And they were strong on secret teachings, knowledge revealed only to initiates who had proved themselves worthy. We know from the gospels how flatly Jesus was opposed to such doctrines and practices. In fact, one scholar very successfully defends the thesis that if Jesus had fallen into the hands of a group like the Qumran community, he would have been condemned to death just as he was in Jerusalem.[6] So in no sense could Qumran or any other desert monastery have been the spiritual home of christianity.

What the wilderness documents show us is simply that the same religious symbolism can have any number of homes. Indeed, if Jesus and the first christians had not drawn on religious ideas that were in the air at the time, the christian message would have had a hard time implanting itself anywhere. The mind has no place to put brand new symbols woven out of whole cloth; our minds are fabrics into which threads are woven one next to another. New meanings, new religious insights can be worked into the fabric, but only if there is a fabric there and a thread to which the insights can be tied.

This seems obvious, and maybe that is why it is so easily forgotten. Christians have too often thought of christianity, its doctrines and its rituals, as a whole cloth which appeared almost out of nowhere. "Conservatives" are then shaken upon discovering that their religion is not at all original when it comes to the forms and concepts and symbols that have been used to express faith in Jesus. But the same mentality of the whole-cloth affects many a "liberal" as well. One cannot expect to communicate new forms of worship, new religious language, new ways of talking about God or praising him, unless the existing fabric has been prepared to receive new threads. New wine cannot be put into old wine sacks; the gospel does call for radical conversion. But this does not do away with the problem of communication, and even radical conversion needs a context wherein the radicalness of God's call can be understood.

This whole problem is not just a modern one. Curious things happened to the christian theology of worship when, as time passed, the jewish origins of the eucharist were forgotten and the eucharistic meal broke off from its historical roots. More of that later.

One final point on the wilderness sect. The Qumran community was extremely clerical and sectarian. It was organized around a group of priests who would have nothing to do with the temple in Jerusalem because they looked upon the temple priesthood of their day as illegitimate. It was also a strictly male community, and no women ever assisted at those meals which anticipated the messianic banquet. But we know of at least one other sect of jewish ascetics, the "therapeutae" or "healers," which included women as well as men. The members of the community all lived in separate houses, seeking solitude for prayer and contemplation; but both men and women met together for common worship on the sabbath. We also know that women shared in the christian eucharist from the earliest times—not a common religious phenomenon in that male and patriarchal world where not even a court of law would accept a woman's testimony. Jesus' own friendship with women, as we read of it in the gospels, was rather unusual, given the cultural and religious atmosphere of the time. Perhaps the first christians' acceptance of women as full participants at its central act of worship owed something not just to Jesus' emphasis on the universality of the Good News, but also to ideas fed into the culture by one or another of those desert communities.

As the various forms of christian life and religious practice developed in the church, christianity came to be the only agency which resisted the greco-roman cultural doctrine of woman's subservience to man. The view of virginity as a "higher" form of christian life has come in for much criticism in recent years—and rightly so, insofar as it implies that virginity is *in itself* a more perfect way of life than marriage. At the same time, we should not forget that the practice of virginity by religious congregations of women was, until very recently, one of the only cultural influences forcing western man to distinguish between woman and sex-object, and above all between woman and mother.

One might ask why the whole thing never developed further, why women could not eventually have presided over the eucharistic meal and thus performed the same roles of leadership as men. There was of course a whole cultural dynamic working against this. The early christians could say with Paul that there is no longer any distinction between male and female in Christ. No distinction in spiritual benefits, that is. Neither Paul nor Jesus himself (none of the Twelve were women) did away with the social and cultural distinctions of the time. The passage of time might have overcome this problem. Deaconesses were very important people in the early church, and the role of these women might well have expanded and evolved further. But such development was short-circuited as the president of the eucharist came to be seen as a "priest," as one who performed a ministry modeled on the idea of Christ as "priest" who did once and for all what the priests in the temple used to do. Chapter 6 will show how the transition from eucharistic celebrant to "priest" depends on the gradual introduction of the symbolism of cultic sacrifice into the eucharistic ritual.

This is not to say that the eucharistic ministry is not a specific ministry—indeed, a ministry so tied up with the essential life of the church that a ritual of ordination came to be required. The christian community needs and wants a covenanted sign, traditionally called "holy orders," a sign which says that the word proclaimed in sermon and sacrament will be the word of God and not simply the word of the minister. But this ministry does not have to be designated by the term "priesthood," which is only a way of interpreting what the minister of the eucharist does. "Priest" is originally an image borrowed from pre-christian cults and applied to Jesus in order to describe his work and mission. When the author of the Letter to the Hebrews makes this application, he knows he is using an interpretative symbol, because he is well aware that sociologically Jesus was not a member of the priestly class (Heb 7:13). What the writer of Hebrews does is to evoke a whole set of symbols and cultic actions, well known to his readers, and use them to interpret the meaning of the salvation accomplished in the layman Jesus. Eventually all this imagery came to be applied to the minister of the eucharist, with some very negative effects. Probably the biggest problem over the centuries has been the view that the ordained minister is "another Christ" in a way that the baptized christian is not. This is simply false, if it means that a man's role gives him an intrinsic value not shared by one who does not perform that role.

Applying to the ordained minister the title of "priest," a title originally given to Jesus alone, has also complicated the role of women in the church. There are enough social and cultural complications (protestant communities which reject "priesthood" as a useful description of the ministry of word and sacrament also have problems with the ordination of women). We need no theological complications! If the eucharistic minister is understood according to the prechristian cultic model of priesthood, and if moreover the image of "Christ the priest" is rigorously applied to the eucharistic ministry, it will be all but impossible to get people to accept a woman in this position.

The problem here is therefore not a theological problem. The "priesthood" of Jesus has to do with the event of the cross, not with his being a male. His humanity has to do with his being human, not with his being a male. The problem is cultural; and christianity, given its historical origins, is bound to have strong resistance against a female priesthood. But the resistance has nothing to do with the theology of "priesthood," any more than male resistance to the equality of women has anything to do, today, with the intrinsic nature of "woman."

* * *

At the last supper Jesus was building on symbols which already had a long and complex history, a history which began at that mysterious moment in time when thought was born and when man began to cash in his ordinary everyday experience and convert it into the stuff of symbolism. His mental images were, as they always are, the means of expressing the most essential human meanings. His most basic symbols were, and are, those which have the most to do with life and death and the critical dividing line between them. "Archetypal" symbols, we often call them. These are the symbols that first and most easily emerge in response to the second question, the human question. From time immemorial, the act of sharing food with another has connoted fellowship, life shared, exultation at being alive. From time immemorial, the image of blood has connoted a "matter of life and death." The shedding of blood radically signifies loss of vitality; so the use of blood in the rituals of primitive man signified his search for life and the preservation of life. When Jesus associated his body and blood, his life and death, with the elements of a communal meal, he evoked symbols which reach back into the origins of man's consciousness.

We can watch the development of these archetypal symbols in the religious history of Israel. The precise meaning of any religious symbol comes from a people's interpretation of their experience, including their experience of the divine. Historically, these experiences are embodied in rituals long before anyone theologized about them. People *did* symbolic things long before they talked about the meaning of their symbols.

The ancient hebrews inherited pastoral rituals from the tribes surrounding them, and when they offered their best lambs or burnt the first-fruits of their fields as a sacrifice to God they were doing nothing new. But after the escape from Egypt, the old rituals acquired a new significance. Chapter 12 of the Book of Exodus, which describes the passover ritual, shows us what happens as further religious experience adds new meanings to existing rites. That chapter deals in detail with the sacrificing of the lamb, the sprinkling of its blood on the doorposts, the preparation of the unleavened bread, and how the lamb and bread are to be eaten. We now have a complex combination of the primitive rituals involving the offering to God of the best of the crops and flocks. The new meaning of it all is defined in the light of the people's experience.

When your children ask you "What does this rite of yours mean?" you shall reply: "This is the passover sacrifice of the Lord, who passed over the houses of the israelites in Egypt; when he struck down the egyptians, he spared our houses." (Ex 12:26-27)

The basic ritual symbols have not changed, but their meaning has been newly defined.

Further experiences add further meanings. Later on, after Moses had received the law on Mount Sinai and the people agreed to do everything the Lord told them, Moses sacrificed a bull. Half of the blood he sprinkled on a stone altar, the other half on the people, thus signifying the covenant between Yahweh and his chosen people. "This is the blood of the covenant which the Lord has made with you in accordance with all these words of his" (Ex 24:8). After that, the people shared a meal together (Ex 24:11).

All of this symbolism comes into play at the last supper. It is pointless to ask how much of it Jesus or his disciples would have been able to articulate in logical language. The symbols evoked by Jesus already had a rich history, and they spoke for themselves. The past experience of the hebrew people, together with the rituals in which those experiences had been incorporated, told them that it is Yahweh who gives life and saves from death, it is Yahweh who gives them their identity as a people, uniting himself with them in a covenant of life. All these abstract words are much more vividly and humanly expressed in the rituals of the sacrificial lamb, the blood of the lamb, the outpouring of blood, the unleavened bread, the sharing of a meal. No matter what sort of meal the last supper was, Jesus' words about his body and blood—about himself and his death and the bread and wine his friends would share in the future—evoked symbols of events which were the common heritage of the jewish people. Perhaps the disciples right then began to grasp more than we usually give them credit for. In any case, it was all a very concrete and definite and, above all, natural way for Jesus to express the meaning of his impending death, a death which he knew lay at the heart of Yahweh's promise of life and a kingdom for his people.

The symbolism of the last supper was spelled out as the early christians reflected on who Jesus was for them. It was spelled out in subtle ways like Mark's formula, "This is *my* blood of the covenant which is to be poured out" (Mk 14:24). This is simply clumsy grammar (in greek as in english) until it is seen in relation to Moses' formula at Sinai, "This is *the* blood of the covenant" (Ex 24:8). There is also the symbolism of the messianic banquet evoked by Jesus' saying, "I will never again drink of the fruit of the vine until the day when I drink it new in the kingdom of God" (Mk 14:25). The idea of a future banquet was emphasized not only in the Qumran ritual meals, but in the thanksgivings of any jewish meal. This was the future time which christians saw as present in Jesus, the time when

the Lord of hosts will provide for all peoples a feast of rich food and choice wines, juicy, rich food and pure choice wines. On this mountain he will destroy the veil that veils all peoples, the web that is woven over all nations; he will destroy death forever. (Is 25:6-7)

Much of this is foreign to the modern mind, because we have so little experience of the richness or depth of symbolism that can be given to a simple meal shared together. It is ironic that we who possess the eucharist, an action which we can call "the summit toward which the activity of the church is directed and the fountain from which all her power flows,"[7] should have lost the *sensitivity toward meals* which alone gives this statement of Vatican II its human foundation. The meaning of the eucharist is not easy to communicate to people whose family meals lack all ritual—meals which, except perhaps for Thanksgiving or weddings or birthdays, amount mostly to eating and running. Religious educators have found that if they can talk people into making one meal a week a real family meal, a ritual meal with a blessing and a sharing of thanks and a cup of wine passed around the table, catechesis on the eucharist becomes easy sailing.

Pastors and religious educators often express a need for new symbols, new images, new ways of getting across the meaning of Jesus and the gospel. There is no question that many of our traditional religious symbols no longer communicate. But it is hard to see how anyone can come up with a more natural symbol than that of breaking bread and sharing a cup together. Our problem is not one of devising new symbols but of working with the radical symbols we already possess. This means, of course, restoring to the christian eucharist some atmosphere of a fellowship meal, whether it be solemnly or simply done. The basic symbolism of the original event is not recaptured when only one member of the community drinks from the cup, or when one needs to make a natural act of faith to the effect that a tasteless little white wafer is in fact a piece of bread.

Some would plead that beer and pretzels or coke and potato chips should replace bread and wine in a truly contemporary eucharist. Much more realistically, oriental christians will ask why bread made from wheat and wine made from grapes should have to be imported into a country where the ordinary "bread and wine" is made from other fruits of the earth. The only religious question at stake here seems to be this: christians should be sure that the choice of food and drink *says everything that Jesus meant*.[8] Once we formulate the question this way, it becomes clear that christianity is after all a historical religion; if we always have to check our doctrinal formulations against the original experience reported in the New Testament, in just the same way our choice of symbolic elements cannot become arbitrary. Once again, it is not a question of new symbols or new symbolic elements. We need to establish the relationship of the few symbols that are still alive for us to a heritage which is much richer than we have often suspected.

Even more basically, our problem is to refurbish the radical symbols that have all but disappeared, not because the *symbols* are defective but because our ability to *think symbolically,* to let the symbols of our religious heritage speak to us, has been clouded over by ways of thinking that leave little room for questions of human and religious value.

4

The Bread and Wine

AROUND THE YEAR 830 A.D. a man by the name of Radbert, who was the abbot of the monastery of Corbie near Amiens in northern France, wrote a treatise for his monks entitled *The Lord's Body and Blood*. The ideas contained in his treatise need not concern us here. In fact Radbert was not much of a theologian; one of his monks, named Ratramnus, did a much better job on the same question a decade or so later. What is interesting is the way the question was posed. Radbert's treatise is the first historical document we possess which approaches the eucharist by focusing directly on the elements of bread and wine. Centuries earlier, men like Augustine and Ambrose and Chrysostom talked about what christians were doing when they gave thanks to God with bread and wine as Jesus did at the last supper. But "with" is the important word here. What the church fathers said about the bread and wine was said in the context of the eucharistic *action*. For Radbert, the starting point was no longer the action but the *elements* out there on the altar table.

Radbert himself was not responsible for shifting the question. By his time the eucharist was no longer an action in which all the faithful participated, and this was bound to affect understanding of the sacrament. Nor was Radbert writing for a religiously sophisticated group of men; many of his monks seem to have been warlords who got into trouble with the emperor and were exiled to the monastery. In any case, we find here a reversion to a primitive religious mentality. Primitive religions all have *sacra,* sacred objects or images which symbolize life and death and for this reason gradually acquire in the people's consciousness a power actually to give life and deal out death.[1] For the people of ancient Crete the bull was such an object, for the canaanites it was the serpent. The hebrews were forbidden to worship a golden calf. But while hebrew religion rejected *sacra* from the animal world, an object like the ark of the covenant at times served the same function in the people's consciousness: it brought them victory when it went before their armies, but when the philistines got hold of the ark it brought them only disease. Christians have attributed this sort of power to crosses and other blessed objects.

As for the eucharistic bread and wine, Paul once blamed the corinthians for engaging in the eucharistic *action* unworthily and for not recognizing the meaning of what they were doing (1 Cor 11). But none of the earliest christian writers described the eucharistic elements as sacred *objects.* It would have been difficult to do so, given the origins of the eucharist in the blessings and ritual actions of an ordinary jewish meal. But by Radbert's time those origins had long since been forgotten. It is possible that the monks of Corbie, whose religious consciousness was much more primitive than that of the early christians, regarded the eucharistic elements primarily as *sacra,* possibly substituting for the sacred objects of some primitive teutonic religion. In any case, Radbert's treatise reflects how the whole manner of regarding the eucharist had shifted from ritual action to sacred object. The shift was perhaps inevitable. A strong case can be made for saying that man, who has never succeeded in running away from archetypal symbols, wants and needs *sacra*. And christian man, once he forgets the ritual origins of the eucharist, will inevitably fasten on the bread and wine as his sacred objects.

By Radbert's time there were already historical factors contributing to the shift. Eucharistic practice had been in decline for several centuries. Few people were receiving communion, and the eucharistic action was becoming the province of the clergy alone. The result was that a cult of looking replaced a cult of doing. The cult of Christ's real presence in the eucharistic elements substituted for the action which at one time had engaged the whole christian community. The practical piety of the faithful once again set the pace for the theologians, and the theology of the eucharist was now destined to split in two. For centuries to come theologians would, like Radbert, start with the bread and wine and develop a theology of the real presence. They would then discuss, as a separate and distinct question, how the sacrifice of the mass is related to the sacrifice of Calvary. The Council of Trent echoed the whole medieval tradition when, some seven hundred years after Radbert, it wrote two such treatises on the eucharist, the second eleven years after the first (1551 and 1562).

We are the inheritors of this tradition, and Radbert's approach has for the most part been ours. Liturgical renewal has made us focus our attention once again on the eucharistic action. But the eucharistic elements remain a preoccupation. Indeed, for a good many christians, understanding of the eucharist begins and ends with the question of the real presence. That question might not be the best question to ask; many centuries went by before anyone explicitly formulated it. But since this is the approach we have inherited, let us take the eucharistic elements and see what happens when we ask our two questions about them.

eucharistic bread and wine
- What is that out there?
- What is that for man?

There is only one answer we can possibly give to the first question, the empirical question. That is bread and wine out there. The only real presence at this level is the physical presence of bread and wine. Some form of magic is needed to sustain any change in the bread and wine at this level, because the physical bread and wine would somehow have to be combined with the physical Jesus. One might insist that Christ is present in his "glorified" body. But at this level of understanding, real presence can only mean physical presence, and the glorified body can be no less physical than the bread and wine. It is simply a body we can't see, and magic or a miracle is still needed to put it together with the eucharistic elements. This physical understanding of the real presence has not been an uncommon one. Historically, as the eucharistic elements gradually became sacred objects, what was known as the *mystery* of the eucharist became a physical *miracle*. As early as the sixth century, we begin to get those fantastic miracle stories which the middle ages thrived on, stories about blood coming out of hosts or the baby Jesus appearing on the paten.

The problem here is not a simple one. Chapter 2 talked about the second question, the symbolic question, as the distinctively human question and the one that brings man into contact with reality even more profoundly than the first. Man has never stopped asking the second question, least of all medieval man who gloried in symbolism. The difficulty is that as attention shifted away from the eucharistic action toward the eucharistic elements "out there," the empirical question entered the scene and became confused with the symbolic or human question. In every culture *sacra* originate as symbols of life and death; they originate as an answer to the second question. But the objects remain what they are at the first level of questioning: they remain serpents or bulls or a cross or bread and wine. The trouble starts only when one begins to assume that a symbolic reality can be dealt with and understood at the same level as an empirical reality.

Today, people tend to look upon symbolic realities as "merely" symbols, "only" symbols. Our particular temptation is to give greater value to the empirical question, and to apply that question to more realities than it is capable of handling. This gives us our own set of problems so far as understanding of the sacraments is concerned. Medieval man was not preoccupied with technology, but he had an analogous problem when it came to discerning the relationship between empirical and symbolic realities. He did not have a set of mental categories that would enable him to distinguish clearly between objects as empirical and those same objects as symbolic. The problem was further complicated by a serious lack of historical knowledge. The medievals were unable to get at the historical origins of existing symbols and rituals, and thus reflect on the process by which ordinary objects and actions *become* symbolic.

In the eleventh century, a man by the name of Berengar reacted against the physical understanding of the eucharist that was then prevalent. His teachings touched off a controversy that became rather ugly on both sides. In 1059 a roman council made Berengar take an oath which illustrates the extent to which the symbolic had been forgotten as a valid category for interpreting reality. He had to swear that "the bread and wine on the altar after the consecration are *not only* a sacramental symbol but the *true* body and blood of Christ, which the priest handles and breaks and which the faithful bite with their teeth." The word *sensualiter* occurs in the last clause, further emphasizing how "true" presence had become identified with *sensory* presence. The only way this council seemed able to preserve orthodox understanding and protect the realism of the eucharistic presence was simply to affirm a physical presence. Thus, the categories which man needs for understanding the sacred had become absorbed into the objects representing the sacred.

During the twelfth century, the concept of "substance" began to come into prominence as a means of explaining the real presence. The development of this concept involves the whole history of medieval scholasticism and its rediscovery of Aristotle's thought. Theologians began asking what happens to the substance of the bread and wine, and all agreed that a change takes place. Explanation of *how* it takes place varied according to one's understanding of "substance" and its metaphysical characteristics. Some held that the substance of bread and wine remains together *with* the body and blood of Christ (the theory of "consubstantiation"). Others taught that the original substances are annihilated and *replaced by* the body and blood (the "annihilation" or "succession" theory). But the explanation which became most prominent was that the substances of bread and wine are changed into the Lord's body and blood, with only the species or accidents of the original substances remaining ("transubstantiation"). The Council of Trent came out in favor of the last explanation, without however going into any discussion of the metaphysics of substance.

What were Trent's options, given the intellectual milieu of the day? Schillebeeckx maintains that the fathers of Trent were not in a position to safeguard the traditional doctrine of the real presence without affirming the particular theory known as transubstantiation.[2] Historically, however, the situation is a great deal more complex. Owing to his very nuanced metaphysics of substance, a theologian like Thomas Aquinas was able to argue for transubstantiation as the only viable explanation of the real presence. But metaphysics was not the real ground on which the discussion took place in the two centuries preceding the Council of Trent.

In 1215 the Fourth Lateran Council had stated in its profession of faith that the eucharistic bread and wine are "transubstantiated." This was *prior to* the major intellectual developments of the scholastic era, and it did not stop theologians from discussing a variety of theories as they went about working out the category of "substance" itself. But eventually, particularly after the thirteenth century, Lateran IV's profession of faith came to be seen as having the force of dogma. Both Scotus and Ockham preferred *con*substantiation on metaphysical grounds; but since the philosophical arguments were not overwhelming on the side of either theory, they had no trouble accepting *trans*ubstantiation, the theory which they understood to be the church's official position. Historically, the connection between the doctrine of the real presence and transubstantiation as the only orthodox explanation of that doctrine came about by ecclesiastical *fiat* and not because of inner philosophical necessity. This is the conclusion of James F. McCue, whose careful analysis of the relevant medieval texts is quite coercive.[3]

At the conclusion of his study, McCue makes some observations which should be kept in mind by any religious educator who has to deal with the theory of transubstantiation. Contrary to the impression common among catholics, Luther had no intention of denying the real presence. But Luther (along with many catholic theologians of the time) held that there was no necessary connection between the traditional doctrine of the real presence and the theory of transubstantiation; and he questioned the church's right to demand adherence to one theory among many. The irony is that in the centuries prior to Trent, the ecclesiastical position to which Luther was objecting had never been formally taken.

Like Topsy, it just growed. The anti-Albigensian confession of faith of Lateran IV was not interpreted as a dogmatic exclusion of all theories of the real presence other than transubstantiation until eighty-five years after that council. Thus what Luther was objecting to would seem to have come about through inadvertance and misunderstanding. Fourteenth and fifteenth century theologians considered themselves bound by a decree which they misinterpreted. This misunderstanding is understandable enough and one could perhaps find other instances similar to this; but the question inevitably arises: is Roman Catholicism to consider itself bound by this series of events? Are theologians of the 14th and 15th centuries and the council of the 16th to be taken as the crooked lines with which God has written straight, or is the Roman Catholic self-understanding and its understanding of the nature and function of dogma such that it can reopen this question in a more basic way than thus far it has done?[4]

Dogmas are expressions of how the church has understood its

faith, and they must be taken seriously. But if we are to take dogmas seriously, we can never read them outside the particular historical contexts in which they were formulated. Nor has any dogma ever carried with it a divine guarantee that it is the *best possible* expression of a point of faith. This is certainly true of transubstantiation, whose status as the official teaching of Trent does not make it the most useful or most adequate teaching for our age. Transubstantiation is an answer to a specific question: how is Christ present in the elements of bread and wine? The problem is whether this is the best question to ask in the first place. To what extent are we to go along with Radbert and the whole medieval tradition which treats the eucharist as an *object*? And, to get behind the various theories of *trans*ubstantiation and *con*substantiation, to what extent is *substance itself* a useful category for understanding the eucharist?

The category of substance originates as an answer to the question "What is that out there?" It is a category basically meant to explain the nature of things like rocks, plants, animals, men and angels. But a sacrament is not that kind of being. A sacrament is a *relational* being—one whose intelligibility, precisely as a being, lies in its relationship to man. This is another way of saying that sacraments exist because man asks the second question, the symbolic question; there would simply be no sacraments if he only asked the empirical question. Now medieval theology lacked the categories needed to deal with the symbolic, with relational beings. It "objectified" such beings and handled them with concepts that belong to and originate from the empirical level of questioning. In explaining the real presence by way of the category of substance, therefore, medieval theology was using analogy. It was understanding a second-question reality by means of a first-question category.

The practical result of all this is an ambiguity built into the theory of transubstantiation itself, or into any other theory that uses the notion of substance to explain the eucharist. The "change" in the bread and wine can be understood as a change at the second level of looking at reality: as a very *real* change, but not one that has to do with the physical order. Our experience of physical change thus provides an analogy for understanding changes that are not physical. The trouble is, we do not usually use the word "change" in this way. When we use it of *exterior objects*, we normally mean some sort of *physical* change: the weather changes, chemical substances change, traffic lights change. It is quite impossible to do away with the ambiguity contained in the statement that "the bread and wine are changed," simply because people naturally understand in a physical way words which originate and are constantly used in empirical contexts. Catechists, beware!

In recent years theologians have brought into play concepts like "transignification" which strive to emphasize that the change is not a physical one.[5] I have heard teachers say that contemporary theology is simply attempting to "translate" transubstantiation and make it meaningful for our age. This is incorrect. It is transubstantiation which is the translation, because the theory uses first-question categories to explain second-question realities. Current theology is returning to categories belonging to the second level of questioning, where the eucharist in fact originated. For behind the entire question of the real presence lies the fact that what began at the last supper as an action came to be treated as an object. The real problem we have to deal with is the objectification of the eucharist and the focusing of attention on the elements out there on the altar.

This problem shows up not only in the language of "change" but in the concepts we have inherited for talking about the "efficacy" of the sacrament. Medieval theology wanted, quite rightly, to show how the grace of any sacrament comes to the faithful through the redemptive work of Jesus and not through human merit. As part of this effort, the objective aspect or "givenness" of the sacraments was distinguished from the human quality of the sacramental celebration. God's offer of grace and salvation, which is expressed and communicated in sacramental signs, was not to be confused with the personal disposition of the minister or of the faithful. God's initiative, in other words, had to be distinguished from man's response to that initiative. This is where the famous expression *ex opere operato* comes into play. The formula came into common use by the second half of the twelfth century, and it was used to handle various questions. It was associated with the question of the minister's morals: as an *opus operatum*, a sacrament has its effect even if the minister of the sacrament is sinful. The same phrase was later brought into discussion of the acts of the recipient. After considering various expressions, the Council of Trent finally opted for this formula in order to affirm what it thought the reformers were denying, namely, that the faith of the recipient is not the only basis for the efficacy of the sacraments.

Any good theologian knew that *ex opere operato* in no sense implies an automatic effect apart from the acts of the believer. The difficulty is that the medieval analysis of the sacraments treats those acts as the acts of one who is no more than a "recipient" of something given. Once the sacraments were objectified, the ritual activity of all the participants was no longer seen as integral to their meaning; and the interior activity of the faithful was largely reduced to a matter of "right intention" or "proper disposition." Any adult catholic will recognize those expressions, which do have a positive meaning, but an extremely minimal one. For this development finally led to a totally negative concept of the recipient's acts. As Scotus saw it, the sacraments are efficacious so long as the recipient "places no obstacle" in the way of their effect.

In this theological climate, with its passive view of man's response to God's initiative, the doctrine of the *opus operatum* came to suggest exactly the *opposite* meaning from that which it was originally intended to express. It fell open to the interpretation that grace is automatically given by the correct performance of a sacramental ritual. Luther quite correctly reacted against the mechanistic implications of this formula. He saw the idea of "placing no obstacle" in the way of an otherwise efficacious sacrament as a denial of the efficacy of faith.

But Luther's condemnation of a formula that had become traditional was too strong for the fathers of Trent, who finally chose to canonize the formula against his denial of it. It is unfortunate that they did not take a hint from Aquinas, who used the formula *ex opere operato* in his earliest work but dropped it entirely in his last writings.[6]

Once again we find ourselves dealing with the problem of how the eucharistic question ought to be formulated. It is one thing to show, as medieval theology did, that the sacraments are spiritually efficacious because of God and not because of man. It is quite another thing to turn an action into a thing, and to reduce the faithful engaged in an act of worship to simple "recipients" of a sacrament correctly performed. When this happens, thoroughly legitimate ritual gestures are bound to acquire superstitious and magical overtones. The problem of magic will remain, I suspect, so long as christians think of themselves as "receiving" the sacraments rather than doing them, celebrating their own identity as christians.

This is more than a matter of sound catechetics and preaching. The smallest gesture communicates volumes. One need only think of the eucharistic words of institution. They are an account of the last supper, addressed to people who are engaged in doing what Jesus said we should do. But as the people became recipients, the words came to be addressed, by the priest bent low over the bread and cup, to the objects to be received. I am reminded of one priest who, shortly after Vatican II, was annoyed at having to celebrate mass facing the people. He had no theological objections to turning the altar around; but at the words of institution he was "distracted from consecrating" by all those people whom he could now see out of the corner of his eye. The theology embodied in ritual and gesture is indeed more powerful than the theology written up in books.

***

Radbert and Trent and the whole subsequent history of eucharistic theology tell us that if we are to answer the question about what the bread and wine are, we have to return to a far more basic way of asking what the eucharist *is*. We have to start not with the objects of bread and wine, nor with the efficacious sacrament and its recipients, but with the action that "proclaims the death of the Lord until he comes," the action that has its roots within the context of an ordinary jewish meal. Our questions then become:

> the eucharistic action   What are we doing?
>
> What do we mean by what we are doing?

The answer to the first question is as simple as it was at the last supper: we are eating and drinking together. As for the second question, the meaning of what we are doing has been *objectively fixed* by the last supper and the death of Jesus. No one who believes in Jesus and who gathers with others to break bread in memory of him can "do this" without of necessity doing it "in memory of me." The essential point of the medieval *ex opere operato* remains: the meaning of the bread and wine are fixed by Jesus and his death, not by my personal faith in him. My faith does not create his presence. His identification of himself with the bread and wine is something given, it is a fact.

But if I am to understand that objective fact, if I am to see any human meaning in what I am doing when I gather with fellow christians to share the bread and the cup, I cannot presuppose my faith in Jesus and then lay it aside as I go about articulating my understanding of what the bread and wine are. The "real presence" is not and never was a substance. That presence makes no human sense, it has no meaning, it has no relation to the human spirit, it is in short unintelligible apart from faith (a second-level perception of reality) in the real Jesus who himself saw (a second-level perception of reality) that the bread and cup would keep telling his followers who he was for them.

This raises another point about our mental models. Some symbols are *like sentences*. They are made up of elements that have independent meanings like words which, apart from any sentence in which they are used, have defined denotations and connotations. Discursive speech—from sophisticated scientific or philosophical language to the everyday language we use to impart information to other people—involves this kind of symbolism. Other symbols are *like a painting or a dance*. There are handbooks of artistic rules governing the balance of color and light and shade used by a painter, or the rhythmic movements of a dancer. But the colors and strokes Da Vinci used to paint the Mona Lisa's mouth have no meaning apart from their relationship to the rest of the painting; that famous smile loses its enchantment if we try to abstract it from the rest of the picture. Nor does any single motion of a ballet dancer make sense apart from the movements that precede and follow.[7]

Sacraments belong to the second type of symbolism. They interweave gestures and objects and words in a complex relationship, so complex that the units which make them up do not have the kind of independent meaning that can be set down in a dictionary. Rituals and sacraments are not discourses. They originate as expressive actions, and it is the action that always remains basic: going into the water or pouring water, laying on hands, anointing with oil, eating and drinking. Indeed, such actions as breaking bread and sharing a cup say what a thousand sentences could not say. But such actions are symbolic in many contexts; so words enter to fix the context and interpret the precise meaning of the action.

The christians of Corinth knew they were meeting for a fellowship meal; eating and drinking together has a radical symbolic meaning in any culture or religion. But Paul had to remind them that because they were meeting precisely as *christians,* their action had a definite religious meaning, one which they were overlooking (1 Cor 11:17-34). He reproached them for behaving rudely toward one another, embarrassing the poor, getting drunk. They were to realize that whenever they met for this ritual meal, they were "proclaiming the death of the Lord," whether they liked it or not. This is why the christian tradition came to attach *words* to the eucharistic *action:* so that the meaning of the action would not slip away and become vague and indeterminate. Eventually christians would come to think of the "consecration" of the mass and "communion" as two separate and even quite unrelated moments. Originally, the whole thing was much simpler: the eucharistic prayer "worded" what the action of eating and drinking together was saying. So for the other christian sacraments. The words and prayers all have to do with relating the particular *action* to the death and resurrection of Jesus. It is in this sense that Christ is the "primary sacrament" whose redemptive work is celebrated in the actions and named in the words of any of our acts of worship.

Medieval theology took account of essential actions and words when it spoke of the "matter" and "form" of the sacraments. But it also treated the sacraments like sentences. It tried to filter out their basic units and analyze the separate meaning of each unit. It is true that the grace of the sacrament, the faith of the recipient, the morality of the minister, and the quality of the celebration are not the same thing. Nor are the bread and wine, some of which can remain after the eating and drinking are finished, quite the same thing as the water that is poured in baptism or the laying on of hands in confirmation and orders. The Mona Lisa's mouth is not the same thing as her eyes or the placement of her hands. There are always basic questions we can ask about faith, or the bread and wine, or the words we say or sing at mass—just as there are basic techniques that enter into the creation of a painting or a poem. But no artist will get very far simply by knowing the elements that make up his art. In just the same way, theology gets into trouble when it forgets that the units of a sacramental action are capable of just so much separate analysis. The lesson of history is that the eucharist loses its bearings and even its relationship to the last supper when its elements—the action, the bread and wine, the faith of the worshipers—are handled like words in a dictionary.

The following chapters will try to pick up the bread and wine out there and put them back into the picture together with faith and people and priests and the death of Jesus.

5

The Cross
and the Eucharist

Wʜᴇɴ ʏᴏᴜ ᴀɴᴅ ɪ are in the process of doing something symbolic, we do not accompany our action with a coldly rational reflection
on what we are doing. A lover who gives his beloved a bouquet of
roses does not, in the act of presenting the flowers, say either to himself or her, "Empirically, my dear, these roses are but one species of
plant life among many others which I might have chosen; but because of the analogy at the symbolic level between their beauty and
your own, I trust you will understand that my gift of these flowers
says something important about what I think of you." To lay out in
rational terms what lies behind a symbolic action often sounds ridic-
ulous, simply because the symbolism is infinitely richer than the logical expression of it. There are surely few christians who, while engaged in eucharistic worship, have consciously said to themselves,
"Empirically that is obviously bread and wine, but for me it means
Christ's body and blood." When we look at the way human aware-

ness really works, it becomes clear that we do not spontaneously know something "out there" as roses or bread and wine, and then *add* an interpretation to our knowledge.

Our *use* of symbols is far more fundamental, therefore, than our *reflection* on the symbols we use. We make and use symbols in a spontaneous way long before we do a logical and reasoned analysis of what our symbols say. And when we finally get around to the analysis, we discover that our symbolic actions still say much more than the analytic language we use to express what symbols are saying. No essay on the nature of love is quite the same thing as that bouquet of roses. This is important. On exactly the same grounds, no dogma on the nature of Christ says exactly what the breaking of the bread says.

Symbols originate as man's means of getting hold of his existence, his *present* existence. When the ancients told stories about the gods and their doings on Olympus before the world began, they were not talking about the past for its own sake. Those stories were explanations of the world of the storyteller's own experience. They explained why there *is* good and evil, why nature *is* fertile, why men and women *now* relate to each other in the way they do. Nor were those stories about the gods and the origins of the world simply told on quiet evenings around the fire. Because they had to do with man's *present* existence, they were solemnly acted out in religious rituals. Christians do the same thing, except that the stories are about Jesus and his forebears (and, unfortunately, the biblical stories are told and re-enacted in a much duller fashion than the ancients would have done).

Still, even though we use symbols because of what they say about our present existence, *ritual* symbols have a unique place in our consciousness. Words and sentences are symbols; rituals are symbols writ large, involving actions and objects, gestures and stories and songs, not just words and sentences. Because of their richness, rituals create a unique intersection between present, past and future. On thanksgiving day, for instance, americans re-enact a ritual meal. Any family which is conscious of the meaning of this feast is giving thanks for blessings in their own lives, not just blessings of the historical past. No story is told as part of the ritual, and yet the past is there. Perhaps the past is *articulated* only by a picture of the pilgrims in the morning newspaper, or among the table decorations, or when one needs to explain the origins of the feast to children. But the past is *evoked* in the consciousness of every american by the very celebration of the feast. The *future* is also there, even when it is not articulated. Thanksgiving, celebrated in homes across the nation at the same time, is saying something about the nation's desire for a future, and about the individual family's hope for the future.

The christian eucharist, seen against this background, is like any other symbolic action. It is not *merely* a symbol but *fully* a symbol. What is unique about the eucharist is not its symbolic status, but rather the reality which this symbolic action reaches and touches and proclaims.

I can sit around a table with my family (I am duly ordained; we talked about that earlier) and celebrate a christian eucharist. I can sit around the same table, with the same people, and pass a cup of wine in memory of my dead grandfather. Assuming that the cup had always been a family ritual at sunday dinner, and assuming that my grandfather was the old-time patriarchal sort of grandfather who might have said "Whenever you pass the cup at future meals you will do it in memory of me," this action would be symbolically identical to the eucharistic action. What is different about the eucharist is the meaning of the action and the reality it reaches. God raised Jesus from the dead and gave him the name that is above every other name. My grandfather has not been given that name, nor does our passing the cup in his memory proclaim the death of one who is named Lord. To say that the eucharist does just this is not to change its symbolic nature; it remains a symbol, our human means of getting hold of our present existence. At the last supper Jesus expressed the meaning of his own existence through a rite which he knew his followers would repeat. The actions done with bread and wine would henceforth be a way for his followers to say that *their* existence and search for the kingdom of God was bound up with himself.

There were other ways to "say" this. The early christians also told stories about Jesus—not just to report what he did for people in the past, but especially to show what is happening now in the midst of the faithful. We have no reason to suppose that the storytellers, the evangelists, were not borrowing from memories of the kind of things Jesus did for people. But their final product was not meant to be a simple report about the past. In *telling stories* about Jesus, the gospel writers were engaged in basically the same type of *symbolic* (and very real) action as we are when we celebrate the eucharist today. Both we and they are saying, in different symbolic forms, what God does for us through Jesus: he heals, he gives life. What the evangelists say through *stories* about what Jesus did for people, we also say through the ritual *action* with bread and wine. Both the stories and the rituals are in their own way interpretations of Jesus; they are different ways of saying who he is for us.

But because story and ritual are also *similar* ways of saying who Jesus is for us, it is not surprising that they would eventually be joined. The rite of the Lord's supper soon came to include lessons from the scriptures and stories about Jesus, in addition to the eucharistic meal itself. The readings and stories were so many different ways of wording what the action with bread and wine was saying in a non-verbal way. Many centuries later, theology would talk about the "presence of the Lord in word and sacrament." This is another way of expressing the similarity between what the gospels are doing when they talk about Jesus, and what christians are doing when they break bread and share the cup. Both are ways of proclaiming that Jesus is Lord and that for us he means life.

"God gave us the sacraments." It is by no means incorrect to say that in our rituals God shares his presence with us. But this presupposes an equally important point which is illustrated by the connection between *story* and *ritual* as complementary interpretations of the meaning of Jesus. If God communicates with us in our rituals or in the words of the Bible, it is because in our rituals and in the written book handed down to us, man is saying something to himself about God. Communication is a symbolic thing, and God does not reveal himself to us apart from the symbols of our own making.

The author of the fourth gospel knew this, and he gave considerable attention to the connection between story and ritual. Modern textual criticism indicates that the final editor of this gospel drew upon various sources and materials. We are certainly not dealing with a single author who sits down and writes about Jesus with a single personal interpretation in mind, the product of one man's mind. Yet despite all the questions one can raise regarding the author's sources, this gospel as it stands gives us a remarkably unified perspective which is most significant for any christian theology of worship. The stories talk about how Jesus gives living *water*, how he brings new *wine*, how he is the living *bread*. We have to be careful not to read medieval sacramental theology back into this symbolism; but the fact remains that many of the stories John tells about Jesus make their point by calling upon ritual symbols to explain the meaning of Jesus. How is Jesus to be understood? What is his meaning for the christian? This is the second-level question which John, like the other evangelists, is attempting to answer. And in order to give his particular interpretation of Jesus, John draws on symbols from the realm of worship known to his readers. In so doing, he gives an important lead to answering important christian questions:

What is the relationship between our eucharist and the cross of Jesus? What does it mean to say that the mass re-enacts Calvary?

John's storytelling technique is different from that of Matthew, Mark and Luke. All the evangelists are of course writing after the resurrection, and their stories about Jesus' miracles and cures have in mind the power of the risen Lord and the faith experience of their own christian communities. But Matthew and Mark and Luke make no effort to explain that this *is* the standpoint from which they are writing. They tell their stories in the first person, relating the event as an eyewitness would. The synoptics occasionally remark that the disciples did not understand what Jesus was doing. But these three writers never step outside the role of narrator, the first-person point of view, in order to tell the reader what the disciples *should* have understood.

John, on the other hand, introduces the third-person point of view in telling his story.[1] He is both a narrator and a commentator. He tells his story as an eyewitness would, but at the same time he will separate himself from the story in order to comment on it. He reports, for instance, that the disciples did not understand the cleansing of the temple or the entry into Jerusalem; he then tells the reader how they *did* understand these incidents after Jesus was raised from the dead (Jn 2:22, 12:16). In the same vein, John keeps interweaving into his stories references to a future event: Jesus' crucifixion, his "hour," the time when his "glory" will be seen. John is quite explicit about not wanting his readers to interpret any of the incidents in his stories apart from Jesus' death and glorification. This means that his readers are to watch for double meanings, because two kinds of understanding are at work throughout his narrative. There is the limited or simply incorrect understanding on the part of the characters in the story. But the reader knows more than those who participated in the events of the story, and John insists that his readers bring their easter faith into play when they read what he has to say. This is the only way the story will be *correctly* understood.

The two kinds of understanding are laid out in a variety of ways. John likes the terms "flesh" and "spirit." *Flesh* sums up the old order, the old law given through Moses, all that is ineffective or no longer effective, now that Jesus has appeared in history. *Spirit* designates what Jesus brings: the new, the effective, the really real. The levels of flesh and spirit also involve two levels of perception, corresponding to many aspects of my "two questions about reality":

namely, seeing the surface of things or seeing merely what is apparent (flesh), as opposed to seeing things the way they really are, seeing the real meaning of things (spirit).

This sounds all very theoretical. It is, compared with the concrete way John makes his point. His whole story unfolds as a dialogue between these two levels of meaning. The dialectic is summed up in the story of Thomas the apostle at the conclusion of the gospel (Jn 20:24-29). Thomas is determined to operate at the level of flesh: he will not believe until he sees and touches the Lord's wounds. Jesus rebukes him by telling him that this level of perception just isn't enough, nor is it ultimately important. It is the people who believe without having to "see" in the manner Thomas insisted on—these are the people who really "see," who really understand the meaning of Jesus and his resurrection.

Thomas is typical of all the characters in this gospel. They all ask questions and understand Jesus at the level of flesh; Jesus answers questions and talks consistently at the level of spirit. In the incident of the cleansing of the temple, the jews talk about a sanctuary it took forty-six years to build; Jesus is talking about the sanctuary of his body. Jesus tells Nicodemus about rebirth through water and the spirit; Nicodemus asks how a grown man can go back into the womb and be reborn. Jesus talks to the samaritan woman about living water that will satisfy thirst once and for all; the woman thinks how nice it would be not to have to come back every day to her well of running water. The crowds are excited over Jesus because they think he is going to provide all the bread they want to eat; Jesus tells them they missed the point, and after he explains about his being living bread and giving his flesh to eat, many left him because they could not understand at the level of spirit. The jews, after excommunicating the man born blind, insist they are not blind; Jesus tells them that at the level of perception which really counts, they are indeed blind.

In short, the supporting characters in John's cast consistently operate at the level of the apparent; they fail to get beyond the first level of questioning. Jesus on the other hand deals only with meaning, faith-meaning, the meaning of events in the light of the resurrection. In John's story there is a near-perfect non-communication between Jesus and the supporting cast. But John's reader is supposed to understand what Jesus means; the reader who possesses the easter faith is equipped to understand the second-level realities Jesus is talking about.

Warned to watch for two levels of understanding, let us see how John works this out as he goes about telling his story. After an introductory chapter which presents the theme and brings the disciples onto the scene, the first part of the gospel (chapters 2 through 12, the "Book of Signs") presents stories about Jesus' works, with lengthy discourses interwoven among the stories, explaining and developing what is going on in the narratives. Laying out the development of John's narrative, with detailed references to chapter and verse, would be long and tedious reading; the gospel is not short, John is repetitious, and many themes are woven together. I shall rely on the reader's general familiarity with the text and use a schematic outline to summarize some of John's main symbolism. The symbols which come into play in worship, and which John uses to interpret the meaning of Jesus, are capitalized.[2]

FLESH, the old, the ineffective. Surface understanding.	SPIRIT, the new, what Jesus brings and is. Real understanding.
At the wedding at Cana, they ran out of wine. There were water jars standing there, WATER used for the ritual purifications customary among the jews.	Jesus transforms the ritual water into WINE. The old gives way to the new, and the transformation is associated with "my hour," the hour when Jesus would shed his BLOOD.
Jesus drove the money changers and SACRIFICIAL ANIMALS out of	Jesus replaces the sacrificial animals and the temple itself. The sanctuary

the TEMPLE. The jews saw the temple as a sanctuary which surely could not be rebuilt in three days.

of which he speaks is the SANCTUARY OF HIS BODY. The "body of Christ" replaces temple worship.

Nicodemus cannot understand how a grown man can go back into his mother's womb and be born again.

The rebirth Jesus means is not a physical return to the womb but rebirth through WATER AND THE SPIRIT.

The samaritan woman draws her WATER out of Jacob's well, running water for which one needs a bucket. (The story is built around a play on words: in greek, the same word means "running" water and "living" water.)

Jesus promises LIVING WATER which will turn into a spring inside the believer, welling up into eternal life. The water of Jacob's well, like the water of purification at Cana, is ineffective.

The paralytic at the pool has lain there for thirty-eight years. The WATER of Bethesda is ineffective.

Like the centurion's son, the paralytic is cured at the WORD of Jesus, who replaces the angel that moved the waters at Bethesda. Anyone who hears his word passes from death to life. The Lazarus story later illustrates how even the graves give up their dead at the sound of Jesus' voice.

The jews wanted to make Jesus king because they thought he would give them all the bread they wanted to eat, just as Moses had given them BREAD in the desert.

It was not Moses who gave them the manna but God; besides, those who ate the bread in the desert are dead. Jesus is the LIVING BREAD given by God. The bread that he gives is himself, his FLESH and BLOOD, for the life of the world.

The jews do not understand how he can give his flesh to eat and his blood to drink.

It is the spirit that gives life, and Jesus' words cannot be understood at the carnal, material level.

The liturgy of the feast of tabernacles included prayers for rain, libations of water, and evoked the theme of life-giving WATER for the nation.

In the context of this feast, Jesus says that anyone who is thirsty should come to *him* and drink. He will provide fountains of LIVING WATER which (as in the Nicodemus story) is associated with the SPIRIT to be given to the faithful.

[Christian baptismal symbolism includes both WATER and LIGHT. The liturgy of the easter vigil makes this connection, but the ordinary baptismal ceremony does not give much stress to the idea of light. In the early church much emphasis was laid on baptism as illumination. John develops this theme:]

The feast of tabernacles also evoked the coming "day of the Lord," ritually symbolized by LIGHT and an illumination of one of the temple courts.

At this feast Jesus proclaims that it is *he* who is the LIGHT of the world. This idea is further spelled out in the story of the man born blind, who receives that LIGHT by washing with WATER at Jesus' command.

In the story of the samaritan woman, Jesus says that the time has come when people will worship no longer on Mount Gerizim or in Jerusalem; they are to worship in spirit and truth. What is this worship? Spirit and truth, as John develops these ideas, refer to the level of perception and understanding which becomes available through faith in Jesus. "Reality" would probably be a more helpful translation of John's term than "truth." In our modern terminology, "truth" tends to refer to abstractions or propositions *about* reality. John uses the word in a much more concrete sense: truth is the new reality which Jesus brings and which the christian grasps through faith.

Worship begins back in the dim moments of archaic time, when men did such things as sprinkle blood on tentposts to ward off demons that could harm their flocks. This ancient ritual was given a new meaning with the hebrews' liberation from Egypt. The ritual of slaying a sacrificial lamb was incorporated into the passover rite; but the blood was no longer sprinkled on doorways, because the ritual was no longer conceived mainly as a protection against the dark forces of nature. The rite now focused on God rather than on demons. It spoke of the Lord as a saving God, a liberator, one who gives his people good things, the best of things, freedom itself.

The passover was not the only ritual which, transformed from a fertility rite, came to express a higher stage of religious consciousness. Just as christianity a millennium later took over pagan feasts like that of the sun-god on December 25th, so the israelites transformed existing feasts in the light of their own religious experience. The festival of pentecost or "weeks" began as a fertility rite performed at the time of the wheat harvest in late spring; it was later associated with Israel's history, particularly the covenant with Noah. Of great importance in the hebrews' early history was the feast of tabernacles. This feast began as a fertility rite connected with the fruit harvest in fall; it came to be associated with the hebrews' own history and the gift of their land, and thus became a time for renewal of the covenant with Yahweh. John's gospel stresses the association of this feast with the coming "day" of the Lord. As time passed, the different feasts acquired additional meanings, so that there were many rituals, including daily rituals of purification, which filled the lives of the people of Israel with reminders of God's gifts to them.[3]

This is the situation John is dealing with, and what his stories are saying is that in Jesus a new and further stage of worship has been reached. For in Jesus God has reached *us* in a new and decisive way. God is spirit, and his spirit is manifested to anyone who accepts Jesus and who, like the man born blind, sees reality in a new and effective way. To worship the Father in spirit and reality (the two terms are for all practical purposes interchangeable) is to worship God through Jesus. The old rituals, the purification rites, the animal sacrifices, the temple itself, are no longer effective. They no longer "work" because they do not designate the new stage of religious awareness that has arrived in Jesus, who transforms all that went before.

The theme of transformation is superbly expressed by Ephraim of Syria, a fourth-century church father, whose commentary on the wedding at Cana uses John's own symbolism to say what these last paragraphs of mine have been saying so prosaically:

The jugs were used for the purification rituals of the jews. Our Lord poured his doctrine into them, to show that he had come according to the way of the law and the prophets, but with the intention of changing everything through his teaching, like water changed into wine. The steward said, "Everyone serves the finest wine first, then the inferior wine." In this way the Lord showed that the old covenant was already a storehouse of provisions, for "the law was given through Moses." But then "grace and truth came through Jesus."

The earthly bridegroom invited the heavenly bridegroom, and the Lord came, ready for the banquet. The guests seated at table invited him who brings the world into his kingdom, and he brought them a marvelous wedding gift. In his richness he did not scorn their poverty. They didn't have enough wine, even ordinary wine, for their guests. And if he had not poured out for them a few of his riches, they would have left the table thirsty and sad. In return for their invitation, he invited them to *his* banquet. . . . Without saying a word, he changed the water into wine. His divine silence awakened his glad heralds, and the steward announced this happy news to the guests; for wine naturally gladdens the heart. Jesus' command made all this happen in an instant, and the bouquet of this wine surpassed the fragrance of any other wine. And so people started asking who was the author of it. . . .

Jesus did not bring with him any strange new creature. He transformed the things that were already there, in order to show he was the master of them. And at the end of time, these same creatures will all be renewed. The will that changed ordinary water into the finest wine with a simple, swift command has the power to give every creature, at the end of time, an inexpressible savor. . . . He started his career by giving to the mouth the taste of his wine, so that he could then attract the ear and lead it to the delights of his savorous teaching.[4]

Ephraim's allegory on the Cana story, which expands the symbolism contained within the story itself, stresses the idea that the event of Jesus is not a break with the past but a further development of it. The old law was good, the wine first served at the feast was good; but Jesus brought the finest wine. (The steward expresses the world of appearances and conventions: one should serve the best wine first. John's story says that in the interior world, the world of religious experience, the best comes after lower stages have been experienced.) John himself, as subsequent stories in his gospel indicate, is much more emphatic than Ephraim about the ineffectiveness of the old, now that the new has appeared. But the essential point remains. Because of Jesus, the old worship is transformed—just as, in fact, Israel's own religious experience had transformed and given new meaning to the ancient fertility rites.

Note that the signs used in worship have not changed. When we were discussing Jesus' action at the last supper, we noted that the bread and wine already had a religious significance, even a messianic significance. The new meaning which Jesus gave to these elements of the meal did not abolish the old meaning but advanced it, concretized it. The fourth gospel works with this same idea and expands it. Christians use the old symbols, but the *meaning* of the symbols has changed because the *reality* they touch is new. Jesus *is* everything the symbols of hebrew worship had been saying. And when christians worship with symbols like light and water, bread and wine, they are saying precisely that Jesus is this "everything" God has promised to man. This last sentence is an abstraction; it becomes concrete and real to you and me *in* the ritual actions we perform with light and water and bread and wine.

***

What is the meaning of the "transformation" worked by Jesus? What is this new stage of religious consciousness that has arrived in him?

This question has to do with the most basic meaning of christian faith as *christian*. John sums up his answer in the words addressed by Jesus to the greeks who asked to "see" him. "Unless a grain of wheat falls into the earth and dies, it remains a single grain of wheat; but if it dies, it brings a good harvest" (Jn 12:24). The *Living Bible*'s paraphrase and expansion of this image is excellent: "I must fall and die like a kernel of wheat that falls into the furrows of the earth. Unless I die I will be alone—a single seed. But my death will produce many new wheat kernels—a plentiful harvest of new lives." The paradox of christian faith, the well-known stumbling block and piece of foolishness, is that life and true union with God is to be found in the death of a man and union with his death.

Christians have heard words like these so often that a certain numbness sets in. We have not been raised as jews or buddhists, and we do not really know any other way to God than the christian way. We accept Jesus; but we do not necessarily go on to ask what makes the phenomenon of a man who died a unique page in the history of religious experience. Some of our own conceptions work against us, particularly the whole notion that the main idea of the christian religion is *life after death*.

That idea is not at all original to christianity. Indeed, christian faith is much less explicit than many other religions about what life after death will be like. Various non-christian beliefs about the reincarnation of souls, for instance, are much more *definite* about the next life than the simple christian image of a new heaven and a new earth where every tear will be wiped away (Rev 21:1-4). And if one is going to believe in the immortality of the human spirit, the theories about absorption into a world-soul are probably more satisfying from a purely rational viewpoint than the overwhelming notion of a personal existence in a new creation.

The mystery cults of the greco-roman world guaranteed life after death, and the greeks of Corinth who converted to christianity had no trouble accepting initiation into "eternal life" through baptism.

They could easily accept Christ as a cosmic symbol. Paul had to remind them that as *christians* their new and eternal life made no sense apart from the cross; the actual death of the man Jesus transformed the symbols of the initiation rites known to the corinthians. The problem is by no means absent today. In the past few decades, we have rightly corrected a false understanding of the resurrection (it "proves Christ's divinity"), but often with a new form of triumphalism that skirts around the cross. "Look, everybody, Christ is alive!" —and his *way* to glory is soft-pedaled in favor of the result, which is much too facilely proclaimed on banners in our churches. If Jesus is victorious *over* death, it is first of all because he is victorious *in* his death.[5]

Christians sometimes conceive of Jesus' life as a kind of horizontal line that starts with his birth and runs through his ministry, then is interrupted or becomes a dotted line for three days between Good Friday and Easter Sunday, after which the solid line is resumed and the cosmic Christ picks up where the historical Jesus left off. This conception is exemplified by the kind of questions sometimes asked about the resurrection. One reads that the risen body of Jesus is a unique body that passes through closed doors or suddenly appears out of nowhere; from this, theologians have gone on to speculate on the qualities of glorified flesh and of the heavenly life that awaits us. This is the mentality of the horizontal line interrupted and resumed, because the question implicitly being asked here is how Jesus' new bodily life (or our future bodily life) compares with the bodily life we now experience. It is probably human enough to ask such questions now and again. The trouble is that such speculations have made their way into a good many catechisms and conveyed to christians a basically *materialistic* notion of the resurrection. The resurrection stories in the gospels are stories of the first christians' experience of the risen Lord; they are not empirical speculations on life after death.

The horizontal line will not do. Our usual physical way of thinking does not work when it is applied to the resurrection. Life as we know it and *Jesus'* life as *he* knew it came to a crashing end on the cross, and that is where the line ends. If Jesus "draws all people to himself," he does so not because he picked up the line of life after a three-day parenthesis, but because the cross at the end of the line becomes a point from which flow out into history the rays of a totally *new* sort of life. There are many things to be debated about the nature and intent of the resurrection narratives, but one would have a difficult time maintaining that these stories are concerned with the material details of Jesus' risen life. It is risky exegesis to try to show that the resurrection narratives do more than "enflesh" the basic kerygma preached by Paul: Jesus is established Lord, raised up and given the name that is above all names, precisely because he accepted *death* (Phil 2:6-11; cf. Rom 1:4). The trouble with the whole horizontal-line view of Jesus is that in such a perspective the cross itself tends to be put into parentheses, as just one more event which is part of the whole package labeled "Christ." We miss the point entirely unless we ask our questions with the understanding that the cross *is* the package.

The fourth gospel is quite explicit (more so than the synoptics) about seeing Jesus' miracles and cures, the doings of his historical life, as possessing a meaning only in relation to the cross. Each of these stories, as they appear in John, evokes the cross, the "hour" of Jesus. The healing of the blind man, the feeding of the multitude, and the raising of Lazarus had, as Dodd puts it, no lasting effect in history. These miracles involved the giving of bodily light, bodily food, bodily life. But the sight of the man born blind would have deteriorated as he got older, the multitude would have been hungry again a day later, and Lazarus had to die again. Such considerations show how useless it is to ask empirical questions of the gospel text (What exactly did Jesus do when he multiplied the loaves? How did he pull off that trick?) when the text is talking about something else. The point of John's stories is that Jesus is the *real* light and bread and life. The stories about him are stories about what Jesus does for the christian *now*, not just for a handful of people in past history. The signs recounted in the fourth gospel are true *for us*, true as present and not past realities, only because of the cross which is *the* life-giving event. The fine wine provided by Jesus at Cana would have run out even more quickly than the inferior wine; the wine he gives now never runs out. The money changers undoubtedly returned to the temple, which in any case was finally destroyed by the romans; the sanctuary of Christ's body is the christian's possession forever. All this is a result of the death of Jesus, his hour, the event that alone enables him to provide the finest wine and to be true light, true bread, true life.

A materialistic understanding of the light or bread or life that Jesus gives obviously does not work. Nor does a materialistic understanding of his death and resurrection. Christian faith does not affirm that life is *resumed* after death. It affirms something much more profound, namely that life comes *out of* death. This is the point of the image about the rich harvest that will come only if the grain of wheat falls into the ground and dies. True, the living harvest comes after the death of the grain; but this is so only because it comes *out of* the death of the grain. This does not imply any rejection of the afterlife. Christians have always taken the moment of physical death seriously; Jesus' preaching talks about the need to make something of our lives before God requires our souls of us. The gospel, however, is much less concerned with the final crunch of physical death than it is with giving us an interpretation of life. It is much less concerned with the material facts of Jesus' own death than it is with his *acceptance* of death as the *meaning of his life* and of the kingdom he was preaching.

When, as John reports it, Jesus washed his disciples' feet the night before he died, he was explaining what typified his own ministry and what kind of service should distinguish anyone who followed him. (Another striking piece of johannine symbolism here. The water of baptism, the water without which "you can have nothing in common with me," is in this episode given the meaning of commitment to service.) At the same time Jesus was explaining his death, his final act of service; for his physical death was his last lesson to his disciples. But since his death wrapped up the meaning of his whole life and ministry, it was much more than a lesson in what to do in the face of total rejection. What Jesus' whole ministry says to mankind is that life and the essential activities of living—being with other people, relating to them, loving and serving them—are tied up with dying. The good news is that Jesus offers a new way of interpreting life and its experiences of death.

So it is that the experience christians are called to live on is the experience of Jesus. That is, ever since the first disciples had their experience of the risen Lord, christians have been using Jesus' experience as a key for interpreting life. Now when christian faith, looking at the Christ-event, issues the invitation to die in order to be alive, it is not saying we should simply make the best of death, whether as physical death or as daily self-sacrifice. This is hardly the "folly" of the cross. Everyday human wisdom tells us we have to make the best of a bad job. What christian faith is saying is that death to self is the precise means through which we experience being alive. We are invited to die to ourselves precisely so that life can be experienced as life. This is the principle that allows our personal faith to be founded not just on hearsay *about* the resurrection, but on concrete experience *of* the kind of life which "resurrected" life is.

John, along with the other New Testament writers, saw this as a new page in the history of religious experience. The event of Jesus simply overturned all normal ideas about the meaning of death and the experience of death. This comes across emphatically in the meaning John gives to the cross. "The son of man must be lifted up as Moses lifted up the serpent in the desert" (Jn 3:14). In order to develop his symbolism of the cross, John reaches back to primitive times, to an incident reported in the Book of Numbers, when the hebrews in the wilderness lost their patience.

They spoke against God and against Moses. "Why did you bring us out of Egypt to die in this wilderness? There is neither bread nor water here; we are sick of this unsatisfying food." At this God sent fiery serpents among the people; their bite brought death to many in Israel. The people came and said to Moses, "We have sinned by speaking against Yahweh and against you. Intercede with Yahweh for us to save us from these serpents." Moses interceded for the people, and Yahweh answered him, "Make a fiery serpent and put it on a standard. If anyone is bitten and looks at it, he shall live." So Moses fashioned a bronze serpent which he put on a standard, and if anyone was bitten by a serpent, he looked at the bronze serpent and lived. (Num 21:4-9)

The story throws us back into the era of fertility cults. The cult of the serpent was apparently quite widely practiced in Canaan, and images of serpents were venerated as sacred objects. (Think of the possibilities for the archaic mind. The snake's characteristics symbolize energy and force: its threatening tongue, the sinuous movements of its body, its method of coiling itself around the victim it attacks. It even sheds its skin, and so for the ancients the snake symbolized the restoration of new life, "resurrection" in its cyclical sense.) Whatever the hebrews of Moses' time may have understood back in the wilderness, the writer of Numbers implies that it was Yahweh who healed, not the bronze serpent itself. Many centuries later, the Book of Wisdom would be much more insistent about this, forbidding any magical or superstitious interpretation of the incident: the people were saved not by what they looked at, but by God the universal savior (Ws 16:5-7).

It is this curious story that John evokes in Jesus' words to Nicodemus about the son of man being "lifted up." The same idea is brought back several chapters later when Jesus tells the unbelieving jews, "When you have lifted up the son of man, then you will know that I am He" (Jn 8:28). John's intention is clear; he wants his reader to identify the power of Yahweh (He Who Is, the divine name revealed to Moses) with the cross of Jesus. The image is fully clarified when, at the end of John's Book of Signs, Jesus explains that "when I am lifted up from the earth, I shall draw all men to myself" (Jn 12:32). These words, John adds, describe the kind of *death* Jesus was going to die.

There is no ascension story in John. For him, Jesus' only journey to the Father is the crucifixion. Jesus' return to the Father *is* the cross, which is at once his humiliation and his exaltation. For John, the process of man's salvation is a "coming down" and a "going up."[7] The process is carried out in Jesus, the word made flesh, who suffers rejection and indignity at the hands of men. But the lowest step in his "coming down," his crucifixion, is also his "going up," his being "lifted up," his exaltation, his return to the Father. The cross is thus an event in two worlds. In the temporal and historical order, Jesus laid down his life for his friends; in the transempirical order, Jesus' self-oblation is accepted by the Father and becomes an event of divine and eternal value. That is, it becomes an event of ultimate *human* value. For anyone who believes in the cross, no distinction need be made anymore between divine and human values. In Jesus, God's world and our own are decisively joined. It is this junction that constitutes a new chapter in the religious experience of mankind. To speak of Jesus as the "god-man" is a very inadequate way of putting this, because it hyphenates what someone like John presents as a union. Much of our inherited religious language implies a kind of opposition between the human and the divine in Jesus; insofar as we create such an opposition in our minds, or attempt to juggle and combine divinity and humanity as separate components, we are doing a poor job of understanding the core of our christian faith.

What the writer of the fourth gospel has done, therefore, is to take a piece of ancient symbolism, the lifting up of a sacred object, and use it to convey the meaning of the death of Jesus. We move once again from fertility cult, through the hebrew realization that it is not objects but Yahweh who saves, to the christian experience that the salvation promised by Yahweh is to be recognized finally in the person of Jesus and in his death. This new stage of religious understanding is reinforced by John's presentation of the crucifixion scene itself. A soldier pierces the side of Jesus, and from his side flow blood and water (Jn 19:31-37). The author emphasizes this detail, arguing against those who were saying that Jesus did not really die, that he was a god who played at being a man, dropping the curtain on the last act and returning to his divine state at the moment of apparent "death." (Recall the episode from the apocryphal *Acts of John* mentioned in chapter 1, where the real Jesus explains the meaning of the cross to the apostle John while the sham Jesus is finishing the show on the cross.)

But there is much more than John's insistence on the actuality of Jesus' death, given the symbolism developed earlier in the gospel. From the physical fact of Jesus' death, the author moves us again to the meaning of that death. In chapter 6, Jesus had spoken of his flesh as real food, his blood as real drink. With his account of Jesus' death, John now makes it clear how Jesus' personal sacrifice—the giving of his body and the outpouring of his blood—could be identified with the eucharistic signs. In the same way, in chapter 7, Jesus had spoken of satisfying the thirst of all who would come to him. John there made one of his third-person editorial remarks, speaking of the "fountain of living water" that was to pour from Jesus' breast, water associated with his glorification and the spirit that was to be given (Jn 7:38-39). With the cross, that water is now given, and along with it the spirit that gives life. In typical johannine fashion, the words referring to the moment of Jesus' death carry a double meaning—a physical meaning and a theological one, very much like the play on words between "running" water and "living" water in the conversation with the samaritan woman. The greek of John 19:30 at the empirical level means simply "he gave up the spirit," he expired, he died. At the symbolic level, the level of human and divine meaning, the same words mean "he gave the Spirit."

John's picture of the crucifixion therefore suggests the following equation:

$$\text{Jesus' death} = \text{his glorification} = \text{the gift of living water} = \text{the gift of his flesh and blood} = \text{the outpouring of the Spirit}$$

What are we to make of this plethora of symbolism, where Jesus' exaltation (indeed his resurrection) and ascension and even the gift of the Spirit seem to be all wrapped up with the event of the cross itself? We are not used to putting such weight on the single event of the crucifixion. We tend to think not with John's mind but with the mind of *Luke*, because it is Luke's symbolism that has been incorporated into the liturgical cycle. The first chapters of the Acts of the Apostles (the second part of Luke's work) contain the familiar ascension and pentecost stories: forty days after the resurrection a "cloud takes Jesus from their sight," and ten days later the tongues of fire came to rest on the heads of the disciples. This is Luke's way of telling about the easter experiences of the first disciples and the birth of the church that resulted from this experience. Luke gives dates, a local habitation and a name, to what went on among the first disciples of Jesus. He is the only New Testament writer to "historicize" the easter experience in quite this detailed way. It was only natural, as christianity gradually became interested in structuring the time of the year according to the events of Jesus' life, that the liturgy should pick up Luke's symbolism. It provided a handy ready-made scheme for an "easter season."

A number of points should be kept in mind here. The original christian "feast" was the Lord's day, *dies dominica*, sunday, the weekly celebration of the death and resurrection of Jesus. It took several centuries for series of special feasts and liturgical seasons to de-

THE CROSS AND THE EUCHARIST 97

velop. That development took place because of man's radical need to give meaning to the passage of time. But there is a danger to be avoided here. If Luke's way of historicizing the experiences of the early church is combined with a materialistic view of Jesus' life after death (the horizontal-line mentality I described earlier), one is liable to fragment the easter experience in an artificial way. Easter Sunday, Ascension Thursday, and Pentecost Sunday are not *historical dates* in the modern sense of the term, like the Fourth of July. The experiences of death, life, and the entry of the Spirit of God into our lives are a composite experience which is played out differently in the history of each of our different individual lives. Luke's scheme structures the experience of the early church. The liturgy picks up that scheme to remind us of the process that should be going on in our lives and to identify our worship—which celebrates what should be going on in our lives—with the total process of death and resurrection.

John himself eventually goes on to tell of the easter event. But he does it quite differently from Luke-Acts. The gift of the Spirit, for example, is given by Jesus himself on the evening of the resurrection. "Receive the Holy Spirit; for those whose sins you forgive, they are forgiven" (Jn 20:22-23). In his resurrection stories John, like the other evangelists, is dealing with the disciples' own experience of the risen Lord, and the effect of that experience on their lives. The stories talk about *their* experience of *him*, not *his own* experience of the new creation. (This should again warn us not to read the resurrection stories as stories about life after death.)

The story of the cross, on the other hand, as John tells it, is the story of Jesus' own experience; and John does not want the story of easter and its sequel—the story of *our* experience—to break loose from the cross. *Prior to* any accounts of the disciples' reaction to and realization of Jesus' glorification and union with the Father, John insists on the cross as the event which contains that glorification and everything which would flow from it, including the outpouring of the Spirit. Good Friday, as John presents it, is Jesus' feast day, the day of his exaltation. Easter and pentecost are *our* feasts, engaging every man's response, in the history of his own life, to the death of the man Jesus.

***

I have been trying to come at John's theme of the cross from many directions, in order to emphasize that christian faith—and any sacramental celebration of it—is rooted in the death of a man and what we make of that death. At our eucharists today, we are tempted to amend Paul's words to read "Whenever we eat this bread and drink this cup we proclaim the death *and resurrection* of the Lord," or some addition to that effect. The addition (which Paul, that great apostle of the resurrection, thought it unnecessary to make) shows our tendency to create a tension between Good Friday and Easter Sunday. Perhaps the life-after-death syndrome comes into play here. The fact is that in proclaiming the death of the Lord we are also proclaiming his exaltation, because the kind of life we call "resurrection" comes only out of death. That is the point which is so hard to appreciate. There is something in us that makes us want to restrict the meaning of the cross to physical death; and this makes the resurrection simply an *after*life.

What kind of life comes out of physical death? Obviously we have no idea, and no one has returned from the grave to describe it to us —not even Jesus. But if death means suffering and conflict and the kind of death to self we have to go through in order to grow as human beings, then we have (or should have) some experience of what life out of death is. The trouble is, we can never define that life in advance. Every such experience is unique and provides us with new answers. And it is within such experiences that we discover the meaning of the resurrection and touch upon "resurrected life."

As John sees it, the orders of flesh and spirit are united in the event of the cross, and the tension between them is overcome. That is, *Jesus* overcame the tension. *We* still experience it. This is evident in the way we *see* things: we have not yet integrated the apparent and the real, the empirical world and the world of values, first- and second-level questioning. (As I mentioned earlier, we also project our perceptions of tension between the divine world and the human world onto our understanding of the humanity and divinity of Jesus. The problem here is in our heads, not in the reality of Jesus.) The tension is evident in the way we *do* things: the struggle between flesh and spirit, the law of our members and the law of the spirit of life in Christ, goes on constantly in our behavior. Jesus' being "lifted up" is God's pledge that integration, wholeness, is possible. And so the christian is called to identify with the process that was carried out in Jesus on behalf of mankind.

Identification with the process begins in baptism. As Paul puts it (Rom 6:4), when we went into the water, we went into the tomb with Christ Jesus and joined him in death. (Our practice of pouring water at baptism "speaks" far less eloquently than the original ritual.) Paul does *not* add that emergence from the water symbolizes resurrection to a new life. The church fathers later expanded Paul's baptismal symbolism. For Paul himself, it was sufficient that baptism be conceived as identification with the *death* of Christ. For him, identification with the resurrection comes *gradually,* as the christian lives out the death to sin symbolized in the baptismal rite. This connection between the cross, baptism, and christian living is beautifully expressed by Leo the Great, a fifth-century church father, who sees the sign of the cross at the center of the christian life:

The process of suffering, dying, and rising again with Christ begins with the mystery of rebirth itself, when death to sin is life for one who is born anew. . . . Those whom the font had taken into its womb as old creatures, the baptismal waters now bring into the world as new beings. But we must still carry out in our behavior what was celebrated in the sacrament. Those who are born of the Holy Spirit cannot control what remains of this world in their bodies unless they take up their cross. . . . The christian, then, must take his stand on Calvary where Christ has brought him. He should direct all his steps to the place where he knows his salvation is to be found. For the Lord's passion is prolonged until the end of time. Just as it is he who is honored and loved in his saints, he who is fed and clothed in the poor, so it is he who suffers in all those who undergo hardship for justice' sake.[8]

A later age would discuss the efficacy of the sacraments in one context and the principles of christian morality in another. In so doing, it forgot the theological profundity of imagery like that used by Leo and Paul.

Now how are we to express the connection between the *eucharist* and the cross? Put in its simplest terms, the eucharist celebrates the cross. But so does baptism, and so do all our sacramental rituals. Many kinds of language have been used to express the uniqueness of the eucharist as the central act of christian worship: the mass is a "sacrifice," it is an action that "renews" or "re-enacts" the saving act of Calvary. Some of this language has proved extremely detrimental, to the point of dividing the christian church at the time of the reformation. In order to get behind these different statements and lay a groundwork for evaluating them, I would propose a frame of reference suggested by the mind of John:

If the cross is a true sign of life and a true junction of flesh and spirit, then what the eucharist says is true and real. The cross *is* what it signifies: Jesus' death *is* his glorification. The eucharistic bread and wine *are* what they signify: they *are* the body and blood of Christ. The same way of speaking, the same level of perceiving and understanding, is involved in both cases. The statement about the bread and wine is not true on the physical plane, any more than Jesus is physical light for the blind, physical bread for the hungry, or physical life for the dead. In their physical selves the bread and wine are *not* the body and blood of Christ, any more than the cross in its physical self is anything more than the death of a man. But the death of Jesus is *more* than its physical self; the bread and wine say more than their mere physical selves. For we are talking about the humanly real, not merely what is empirically real.

At that second level of perception, christian faith sees that the event of the cross brought about a union between God and man. The Father accepted Jesus' total gift of himself, and this we believe constituted a definitive relationship between God and man. This is the "efficacy" of the cross. Celebrating the eucharist brings about a union between God and ourselves, but only in proportion to our response: the Father accepts *our* self-gift insofar as we give it. This is the "efficacy" of the eucharist.

The cross is, for Jesus, a sacrament of union with God. The eucharist is, for us, the sacrament of a union which has not been fully accomplished. Jesus' historical life ended in union with the Father. Our historical lives are meant to end in the same union. But as we work out our historical lives, we are to serve and heal, unify and reconcile as Jesus did. Our eucharist is a covenanted sign that union with God is possible, that the spirit of God is at work in us as in Jesus, and that our own efforts at healing and reconciliation will not be in vain.

On the cross, one man died to "gather together in unity the scattered children of God" (Jn 11:52). In the eucharist, there is bread broken, a cup of wine shared. Bread made one, harvested from scattered grains on the hillside, bread which tells of a body given for the life of the world. Wine made from grapes taken off the branches of the vine, he the vine, we the branches. Anyone who proclaims Jesus' death by eating the bread and sharing the cup commits himself to the work of unity, to the work of making a body.

The thing which becomes a symbol retains its original form and its original content. It does not become, so to speak, an empty shell into which another content is poured; in itself, through its own existence, it makes another reality transparent which cannot appear in any other form.[9]

Those words of a modern jewish writer bear re-reading, particularly when we are tempted to make of the finite something other than what it is. Think of the cross. Then think of the eucharist which celebrates the cross. They are two "things," an event and a ritual action which have become symbolic and therefore divinely and humanly *real* to us, without becoming anything more than what they are: the death of a man, a piece of bread, a cup of wine. The death of that man, without becoming anything other than what it empirically is, says life. And the bread and wine, without becoming empty shells into which another content needs to be poured, are our way of sinking our teeth into the mystery of the cross.

6

Symbol Upon Symbol

A la recherche du temps perdu. A few pages of nostalgia for old and not-so-old catholics.

The time was when the big hurdle for the budding altar boy to overcome, before he could graduate to service at the altar, was memorization of the latin prayers. *Et cum spiritu tuo* and the like were of course easy. But for some reason the answer to the *Orate fratres* was a tough one; the end of the *Suscipiat* was a real tongue-twister for a ten-year-old: *ad utilitatem quoque nostram totiusque ecclesiae suae sanctae.* Still, the priest would wait for you to finish that one; and in any case, you started reciting it while he was still saying the rest of the *Orate fratres.* The prayers at the foot of the altar were much more of a challenge, where you had to dialogue the verses of Psalm 42 with the priest. In those days you judged the quality of celebrants on how much time they'd give you to squeeze in the *Quia tu es Deus fortitudo mea*'s and *Spera in Deo quoniam adhuc*'s. Some would never wait for you; they'd even cut you off in the middle of the *Confiteor*. You were really a seasoned server when you could get all the prayers in without skipping anything, no matter how fast the priest went or how loud the music was (a high mass complicated things). This gave you even more status than being able to carry the missal from the epistle side to the gospel side without looking as though the thing was too heavy for you, and without tripping on your cassock as you genuflected at the bottom step. (The good priests were the ones who gave you a nice clear hand-signal to let you know they had finished the epistle.)

But in any case you got plenty of practice with the *Confiteor* because you recited it twice at every mass—at the beginning and again before communion. For the most part, anyway. Before you started the *Confiteor* at communion you had to look out into the congregation (that was a big moment which could be carried off with varying degrees of ostentation) to see if anyone was actually coming to communion. Rarely were there any communions at funerals or weddings, and sometimes not at the sunday noon mass. The early risers catching a late mass had eaten breakfast, and the late risers had undoubtedly eaten or drunk something after midnight (besides, just laughing at a dirty joke at that party the night before was enough to keep you from communion). It was at the late mass, too, that many more people left before the end of the mass (you fulfilled your obligation by staying for the priest's communion). But you had to get out before the priest turned around, came down the altar steps and began the prayers for the conversion of Russia. Maybe staying for these prayers, once you were caught, had something to do not so much with poor Russia but with the fact that the prayers after mass were, after all, the only prayers recited by the congregation.

During the 1950's liturgists and theologians were talking about the possibility of changes in the mass. Momentum was given to these discussions by the revision of the holy week ceremonies which began to take place in the mid-fifties. The new order for these services (simpler ceremonies, restoration of the easter vigil) made it clear that the Roman Missal, whose regulations had been left quite untouched since 1570, was not sacrosanct. At a liturgical conference at Assisi in 1956, many bishops recommended use of the vernacular at mass; at least one urged that the eucharistic fast be reduced to three hours for morning masses, as had already been done for certain evening masses. The communion fast was in fact changed by Pius XII in April 1957: three hours for solid foods, one hour for liquids, and water no longer broke the fast. But the thought of any vernacular at mass was a hard pill for many to swallow. One of John XXIII's first official acts was to issue an encyclical reaffirming the importance of latin and insisting on its use in seminary lectures. Latin was a universal language, many argued, and use of the vernacular at mass would lead to nationalism and isolationism; it would prevent the spread of catholic worship and of the universal message of Christ.[1]

Then Pope John called his council, but few people thought much would come of it. Cardinal Tardini, the Vatican secretary of state, summed up the attitude of many when he said, "It will not last long; we shall already be agreed on many things by the time the council opens."[2] He also added that there would be no discussion on reform of the liturgical calendar. In 1960, not long after Tardini's statement and fully two years before the first session of the council, Rome issued a substantial reform of the calendar. The complex rankings of feasts (the old doubles of the first or second class, double majors, semidoubles, and all that) were simplified, many vigils and octaves and complicated commemorations were dropped, and "high" and "low" mass gave way to more flexible norms for "sung" and "simple" masses. Such reforms were a great relief for many priests, organists and choirmasters who had never managed to figure out the old system anyway. What the faithful in the pews noticed was that the *Confiteor* before communion had been dropped. Maybe Tardini and others thought this would take care of liturgical reform, and the council wouldn't have to bother with it.

The bishops of course thought otherwise. Their first decree, issued late in 1963, was the *Constitution on the Sacred Liturgy*, a broad plan for liturgical reform which was to be implemented in the years to come.

Dialogue masses (in latin) and various other forms of congregational participation had already begun to spread more widely in the early 1960's. A really up-to-date congregation knew how to sing not only the latin responses but even a few chant masses. The only official liturgical change between 1960 and 1964 came when, in 1962, Pope John inserted Saint Joseph's name into the list of saints in the canon of the mass. Archbishop Grimshaw of Birmingham felt that this bold move was "more than one had dared to hope for." (It was later noted, in a source I no longer recall, that this happened shortly after Cardinal Ottaviani had told the council that no matter what liturgical changes the fathers were to make, the venerable roman canon, unchanged for well over a thousand years, must surely remain untouched. The manner of Pope John's response—if that is what it was—was not out of character.)

In April 1964, catholics had to start changing their communion habits, answering *amen* to the priest's words, *corpus Christi*. One actually had to *say* something before sticking out one's tongue to receive the host (many people, until they got the new procedure down pat, would get nervous and snap at the host). But by the end of the year the priest was saying "The body of Christ," and one could answer "aay-men" instead of "ah-men." For on the first sunday of advent 1964, several weeks after Lyndon Johnson defeated Barry Goldwater in a landslide election, american catholics went to church and faced their first official half-english half-latin mass.

There was much shuffling of papers as the congregation read prayers and responses in english, while the priest shifted back to latin for the orations, the canon, and all prayers recited by himself alone. No one had to learn english responses to Psalm 42, which was dropped from the prayers at the foot of the altar, along with the last gospel and the prayers after mass. One could set the papers aside at the epistle and gospel (unless there was a poor reader) and at the Our Father (unless some ambitious liturgist was trying to get you to sing it). It would be at least another six or seven years before the average parish had to cope with the greeting of peace. But in any case, for all the distraction, you could at least come to church and receive communion, even at an early mass, with a good breakfast under your belt. In November 1964, Pope Paul had reduced the eucharistic fast to one hour.

There was much left to be desired here. Everyone sensed that the mixture of languages was a compromise, an interim measure—and a clumsy one at that. Even more basic was the difficulty a great many people experienced in shifting from mass as private devotion to mass as communal expression. Why couldn't everyone "follow the mass" in their own private way, using their missals as they always had? In 1964, "some of the traditionalists among the clergy are beginning to wonder just how far 'togetherness' and 'participation' can lead us. It appears that some of the scholars will not be content until the laity are breathing down our necks at Mass and getting underfoot at the Lavabo."[3]

Altars were being turned around by this time. For some this meant embarrassment or self-consciousness at finding oneself "staring directly into the eyes of the priest."[4] Nor did many priests find it easy actually to *look* at people when greeting them "The Lord be with you." The ingrained habits of years had to be broken. A still more difficult re-programing of rubrical automatisms was called for in May of 1967, when a roman instruction eliminated numerous genuflections, altar-kissings, signs of the cross over the offerings, and the need to keep thumbs and forefingers joined after the consecration. The same month brought permission, at long last, for the latin canon to be recited aloud, and for vernacular translations of the canon to be prepared. (The avant-garde meanwhile, not content with the roman canon, were actually asking for new eucharistic prayers.) Saturday evening masses were officially approved, along with the practice of receiving communion standing. (What will become of our marble altar rail?) Experimental weekday lectionaries had been in use for awhile in many places, and the daily mass-goer no longer had to listen to the parable of the wise and foolish virgins three times a week.

The forms and formulas of the old Roman Missal were no longer sacred. But using anything other than official translations and approved formulas still seemed quite daring in the late sixties. Celebrations done in a style which has now become normal and accepted, even in parish churches, were in those days known as "underground" liturgies. Helicon Press in 1968 brought out a little volume called *The Underground Mass Book,* containing such shocking things as alternative eucharistic prayers, guitar hymns, and readings on social or human concerns excerpted from contemporary writers. Meanwhile, back at the parish church, ordinary sunday mass-goers were coping with what seemed to be ever-changing translations of texts and new hymns (What ever happened to our beautiful choir?), commentators who were forever telling them to stand or sit or kneel, and pastors who were reluctantly introducing the latest liturgical orders from the bishop without very often explaining *why.*

In the spring of 1969 the new lectionary was completed, with its three-year cycle of readings for sundays (it seemed priests would really have to learn to preach on scripture). At the same time the new Order of Mass was published, giving a framework which would not need substantial alteration in the near future. Plenty of room was left for the addition of alternate prayers; and the rubrics frequently call attention to the need for flexibility, adaptation and imagination.

Like a similar commission some four centuries earlier, the many scholars who collaborated on these new liturgical books could hope that their efforts would be "well accepted and approved by all sober, peaceable, and truly conscientious sons of the church"; but of course they could not expect "that men of factious, peevish, and perverse spirits should be satisfied with anything that can be done in this kind by any other than themselves" (from the preface to the anglican *Book of Common Prayer*, 1552). Since 1970, there has been some factiousness in parishes which have not yet learned that different styles of liturgy are needed for different people, and that not all the sunday masses need be alike. Then there are the perverse spirits who have been agitating for communion in the hand. And as for peevishness, it is evident to all that not even the best liturgical texts in the world can turn a bad celebrant into a good one, or a poorly planned and poorly executed liturgy into an exciting religious experience.

* * *

There are two sorts of symbolism connected with the eucharist. The first I would call *primary symbolism*. This includes the action of eating and drinking and whatever words and gestures articulate the *basic* meaning of the ritual meal. Then there is *secondary symbolism*, the symbolism built up around the inner primary core and intended to enhance it. Most of the elements in the ritual of the mass, taken by themselves, are secondary symbols. The primary meaning of the eucharist is given in the action of eating and drinking, and in whatever symbols are used to "word" the action, to say that in this particular action we are "proclaiming the death of the Lord until he comes." The christian tradition has at some point normally used a verbal formula in order to make the meaning of the action as explicit as possible. But the eucharistic ritual in fact contains many kinds of "language"—prayers, readings, processions, gestures, music, color, dress, the arrangement and design of the church building itself—all meant to point to and lead the participant into the primary core.

Taken singly, most of the ritual actions and symbols mentioned in my survey of liturgical reforms are arbitrary and not essential to the eucharist. But the *composite* is by no means arbitrary. Most of the liturgical changes over the last decade or so have had to do with eliminating secondary symbolism which detracted from the primary, and replacing it with ritual activity which would once again focus in on the core. Most of the symbolism of the old roman rite was calculated to call attention to the *objects* of bread and wine; the new rite stresses the *action* of a faith community which is celebrating its redemption. The latter is a much more difficult thing to handle than the former. When the ritual is built around the idea of action, and there is in fact little or no engagement on the part of the participants, the only result is dullness and wordiness. People who prefer to be spectators at a rite and priests who do not really want their parishioners engaged in the ritual would probably be better off with the old tridentine mass. It at least guaranteed, in the unfolding of the rite, a central object which one could focus on. I could contemplate and receive the body of Christ without having to come to terms—at least in church—with the body of Christ which is my neighbor next to me in the pew.

The importance of secondary symbolism and its influence on the primary is well summed up in the complete shift in attitude toward the tabernacle (the body of Christ "out there") which took place over a period of just ten years. Back in 1957 it was decreed that mass should be celebrated on the altar where the eucharist is reserved; a church having only one altar should have the tabernacle on that altar. In 1964 it was decreed that the eucharist *could* be reserved on the main altar *or* on a truly prominent side altar; masses could be celebrated facing the people *even with* a tabernacle on the altar. By 1967 the full circle was turned: the tabernacle should *not* be on the eucharistic altar; in fact, it should ideally be placed not even in the sanctuary but in a chapel distinct from the central part of the church.[5]

Along with this development came the gradual disappearance of crosses standing on the altar. When altars were first turned around, it was felt that there must be a crucifix on the altar. Some church-goods stores even came out with crucifixes which had a corpus on either side of the cross, one facing the priest and the other facing the people. Historically, as Dix notes, the placing of anything whatsoever on the altar except the bread and cup for the eucharist was "entirely contrary to normal christian feeling" until around the ninth century. This included not just tabernacles and altar crosses but even candlesticks, which were originally placed around or beside the altar but not upon it.[6]

Thus what we have seen over the last decade is a correction, by primary symbolism, of the secondary visual and even architectural dimension of eucharistic symbolism. The eucharist as object, a conception which became ritually supreme during the second millennium of christian history, had at last to bow to the eucharist as action.

The problem of benediction and the "cult of the real presence" obviously arises here. The catholic tradition will have to keep re-evaluating its practice in this area, just as it has gradually (and even rapidly) changed other secondary symbolism in line with a restored eucharistic theology. It would be foolish to condemn a ritual like benediction out of hand. Such condemnation would ignore the reality of history and the christian people's search for self-understanding in different eras and cultures. The practice of reserving the eucharist goes back to the earliest times, when the faithful would take eucharistic bread home with them to make their communion on mornings when there was no liturgy. The bread was also taken to those who were absent from the sunday liturgy. There is no historical or theological reason why the eucharist, when reserved in churches, should not be reserved in a setting of dignity and beauty. Trouble arises only when an elaborate cult gets built around the reserved sacrament, and that cult comes to detract from or virtually replace the eucharistic action.

Historically even such aberrations had their positive side. The protestant reformers rightly wanted to do away with the superstition and idolatry which had grown up around the sacrament of the altar. But as the history of the reformation churches unfolded, most of them all but lost the eucharist; the Lord's supper came to be celebrated only a few times a year. The eucharistic *action* was, in different ways, virtually lost to protestants and catholics alike. For all its distortions, the cult of the blessed sacrament did keep the eucharist alive as a primary christian sacrament, and one must be careful not to judge a ceremony like benediction too harshly. As for the future, I would only point out that a ritual like benediction involves secondary symbolism; if it is to be retained, it cannot be allowed to lose its roots in the primary meaning of the eucharist. This is not an easy thing to manage ritually and symbolically, as history has shown. And this may explain why benediction has entirely disappeared from the religious practice of many catholics who have learned to experience the eucharist as action. I suspect that the practical piety of the faithful will solve the problem of the cult of the real presence, just as that piety originally created the problem. The job of catechists and preachers is to help the faithful form their piety along the lines of a critically sound eucharistic theology.

The distinction between primary and secondary symbolism is extremely important for interpreting the eucharistic language we have inherited. Take the terms "real presence" and "consecration." These ideas will mean one thing when we are talking about sharing the bread and cup in memory of the Lord. The meaning will change, however, if it comes out of secondary symbolism, particularly the kind of secondary symbolism which led to the development of the object-mentality.

It is hard for us today to think of the "real presence" as anything but an objectified physical presence, because use of the expression and the meaning of "real" in that context has been so tied up historically with the eucharist as object. In recent years theologians have been emphasizing that Christ's eucharistic presence is a *personal* presence, a type of presence which is humanly much more "real" than mere physical presence. I can be physically present in a room with you without being personally present to you; indeed, I can be personally present to someone I love even when I am physically absent.[7]

Once we return to primary symbolism, the idea of the eucharistic "presence of Christ" basically becomes a way of symbolizing the connection between our action and the Lord whose victory it celebrates. Luke's story of the disciples at Emmaus is a good example of what the "real presence" means, prior to and apart from objectification of the eucharistic elements: the risen Lord is in the midst of his people, and he is recognized in the breaking of the bread (Lk 24:13-35). If this presence is what we call a mysterious presence, it is no less mysterious and no more objectifiable than the personal presence of you or me to someone we love. People can even *make* love without being present to each other. At the level of primary symbolism, the kind of presence of which the eucharist speaks cannot be laid out on a table, any more than you or I can nail down and take hold of what makes another personally present to us, least of all in intimacies like the act of love. We can say a great deal about what personal presence is *not*, but we can never objectify everything it *is*.

The notion of consecration is closely related to that of presence. One might ask the classic question, "What happens at the moment of consecration during mass?" Put this way, the question draws us back into the object-mentality, because what the question really means is, "What happens to the bread and wine when the words of institution are pronounced?" At the empirical level *nothing* happens to the bread and wine, as any chemical analysis would demonstrate. (Such an analysis was attempted, with no result, back in the nineteenth century; even so recently as the late 1950's there was a debate over the viability of interpreting the eucharistic "change" as a change in the arrangement of molecules, electrons, etc.[8]) The *sense* of the question about "consecration" has nothing to do with a magical moment involving an empirical transformation of elements. What then does the idea of consecration mean in connection with the eucharist?

Once again the gospel of John is helpful because it provides a primary core meaning for the idea, a meaning directly associated with the event of the cross. John uses two traditional liturgical terms to describe the work and mission of Jesus. Early in the gospel Jesus tells his disciples that his food is to do his Father's will and to "complete" his work (Jn 4:34); the works his Father has given him to "complete" testify that the Father has sent him (5:36). In the priestly prayer, which is uttered from the viewpoint of the crucifixion already having taken place, this work is declared as finally "completed" (17:4). The theme of completion is evoked once again in John's picture of the crucifixion. In Matthew and Mark, Jesus utters a "loud cry" before he dies (Mt 27:50, Mk 15:37). Luke makes that cry a prayer: "Father, into your hands I commend my spirit" (Lk 24:46, quoting Ps 31:5). John makes it a theological statement: "It is completed" (Jn 19:30). The expression gets its meaning from the themes mentioned earlier in the gospel.

But what is interesting is that the greek word used here *(telein)* also has a liturgical meaning. The word is quite extensively used in greek literature to refer to the performance and "completion" of a sacred rite; a "completed" person was one who was now consecrated to a god and initiated into his mysteries. It is not unlikely that the evangelist had this connotation in mind when he placed the word on Jesus' lips. For in the priestly prayer of Jesus, John uses a second liturgical term to describe Jesus' self-oblation: "For their sake I *consecrate* myself so that they too may be consecrated in truth" (17:19). What John is suggesting, therefore, is that Jesus' death is the completion of a sacred rite.[9] This symbolism goes hand in hand with what we saw in the last chapter. Just as Jesus' death changes the meaning of religious symbols like bread and light and water, so his death gives a new meaning to the ancient idea of ritual consecration and sacrifice.

If we follow John's lead and prescind from later historical and theological developments, the meaning of "consecration" becomes quite simple. The "moment of consecration" is the death of Jesus; what our eucharistic action does is to celebrate *that* moment. There is no need for any further moments of consecration except the ones that take place in our own hearts. The words of institution, along with other words used in the eucharistic ritual, articulate the meaning of our action. They affirm the connection between this action, this moment, and the moment of the cross. The narrative of the last supper acquired liturgical importance precisely because it *states* a meaning which was actually *given* in the event of the cross.

Even so, the institution narrative acquired its importance only gradually. There are very good historical indications that the account of the last supper did not become a regular part of christian eucharistic prayers until sometime during the second century. The earliest christians probably "worded" their eucharist with a series of thanksgivings modeled on the jewish thanksgiving prayers used at ritual meals. (See the prayer quoted at the beginning of chapter 3.) Specific reference to the last supper developed later, as christianity separated more and more from judaism and as the need developed to state the specifically christian meaning of the eucharistic meal.[10]

Paul gives an account of the last supper in 1 Corinthians 11. This was probably not a liturgical text, not a text used in the eucharistic action itself, but a piece of *catechism* to be learned and kept in mind during worship because it interprets what christians are doing when they gather for their ritual meal. If the christians at Corinth were actually *using* a narrative like this one in their gatherings, why should Paul have to remind them of it in such detail? They could forget their catechism, but it is most unlikely that Paul would have had to repeat a text which they heard every time they met for the breaking of the bread.[11] The first christians did what Jesus *did* at the last supper; they were not immediately concerned with what he *said*, even though they knew from their catechism what he said. Paul had to remind the corinthians of what he had taught them because they were forgetting the indissoluble connection between their meal and the death of Jesus, a connection Jesus had affirmed at the last supper.

The first christians, in short, did not think in terms of *words* of consecration. For them the eucharist was an *action* of consecration, because what the action bespoke was the consecration that took place on the cross. As for ritual words, the thanksgivings of the jewish ritual meal—repeated and further embellished with christian ideas—would initially have been quite sufficient, particularly in an era when the sharing of the bread and cup had not yet been separated from a larger meal.

In this connection I would again emphasize a point made in chapter 1, namely that a good many of the early christians knew little about the life of Jesus beyond the basic facts of his death and resurrection. Throughout the letters of Paul, which are our earliest christian documents and which antedate the written gospels, there is no concern with the historical ministry of Jesus. Candidates for baptism received instruction not on the historical life of Jesus but on the points that we find stressed throughout Paul's letters: Jesus' lordship, his redeeming death, the kind of conduct expected of a christian. But once the written gospels were formed, and particularly after they came into general circulation during the first half of the second century, a new trend began developing which would have great importance for christian worship. Dix emphasizes a point which is too easily forgotten by modern christians who have grown up with the gospels. We must not forget "the immense difference which the circulation of written gospels must have made to the way in which christians regarded the historical origin of their faith, and to the store they set by detailed allusions to it."[12]

As interest in the historical life of Jesus developed, accounts of the last supper would have become a more and more natural way of wording the eucharist. But the process did not stop with the mere addition of an institution narrative to a series of thanksgivings modeled on jewish practice. The church was also losing contact with its jewish origins, and this would necessarily affect its understanding of the eucharistic action. Following the jewish model, christians could recite a series of thanksgivings for the works of God and for the work of redemption wrought in the person of Jesus; and such prayer would have been seen as quite sufficient for expressing the new meaning of an old ritual, a ritual now done "in memory of me." But by the third century, this was no longer an adequate way of wording the eucharist. Looking at the texts of this era, we find that once the historical reference to the last supper had been introduced or elaborated, the eucharistic prayer came to acquire a new focus or center.[13] The focus was now the institution narrative and the material built around it, including invocation of the Holy Spirit to transform the bread and wine.

There is of course no reason why christian prayer should not have its own history, its own evolution; there is nothing sacrosanct about the forms of jewish prayer. But once again, if the origin of the eucharist and therefore its *primary* symbolism is tied up with a ritual meal and the relationship of that meal to the death of Jesus, then the *secondary* symbolism which is built into the surrounding rite must not be allowed to lose sight of these origins. The words of institution are by no means opposed to primary symbolism; on the contrary, they affirm it. But as the account of the last supper and the invocations surrounding it gradually became the *center* of the eucharistic prayer, *displacing* the original idea of thanksgiving (which was eventually confined largely to what we call the "preface"), there also developed a type of secondary symbolism which would become more and more troublesome.

Chapter 4 discussed the object-mentality which was the end result of this development. We should now see something of how this occurred. This is not the place for a history of the liturgy, which would have to pick up with the gradual separation of the eucharist as such from the agape or fellowship meal, and go on to detail the evolution of ceremonies through the centuries. I want to highlight only those developments which throw light on the eucharistic language and theological concepts we have inherited.

***

John's gospel evokes sacrificial imagery along with the many other ritual symbols to which the author sees a new meaning given by the death of Jesus. The Letter to the Hebrews, a late New Testament writing, picks up the same theme and develops it at length: the old animal sacrifices, which in any case were only provisionally effective, are now no longer effective at all, because the ultimate sacrifice, the decisive reconciliation between God and man, has taken place in Christ Jesus. The imagery of sacrifice, which originated in ancient rituals dealing with the death of a victim or the destruction of an offering, thus came to take its place alongside other symbols interpreting the death of Jesus—such as John's "lifting up," or his image of the seed dying in the ground in order to bring forth life in abundance. As I shall emphasize in the next chapters, the concept of sacrifice has no fixed meaning; it means different things at different stages of religious consciousness. But the concept evokes an action in which men and women have been engaged since the dawn of mankind, whatever they may have understood by the action. So it is that the language of "sacrifice" was destined to become a powerful tool for conveying the meaning of what Jesus did, what *his* "death and destruction" meant.

Since the eucharist celebrates the cross, it was only natural that imagery applied to the cross should eventually be applied to the eucharist. This happens very early, even before the end of the first century. The *Didache* calls the eucharist a sacrifice, and the *First Epistle of Clement* associates the eucharist with the cultic ideas of priesthood and sacrifice that had been applied to Jesus himself by the author of Hebrews.[14] Clement also insists on the old cultic distinction between priesthood and laity (this is the first extant document which uses the word "layman"). Ideas stemming from the wilderness sects may also have been operative here, at least in some churches, from the earliest days of christianity. Qumran's ritual meals of bread and wine were presided over by one called a "priest," and those meals substituted for the temple sacrifices conducted by priests whom the desert sects considered illegitimate.

Given the religious ideas that were in the air at the time, the application of old cultic and sacrificial imagery to the eucharist would have been a natural enough development, not in itself unfaithful to the meaning of the cross or the intention of Jesus. The distinction of roles in any sort of community is a sociological reality. The gospels make it clear enough that Jesus was opposed to *caste distinctions* based on roles (see Mt 23:1-12 for a strong statement of this). But it is equally clear that his followers would and did perform different functions within the community. It is one thing for different people to perform different functions within society; it is another thing (though unfortunately a very human thing) for a group to "sacralize" a person because of the role he or she plays. It is one thing to attach the very ancient idea of sacrifice to the eucharist as a means of interpreting this central act of christian worship. It is quite another thing to bring back the ritual forms and caste distinctions associated with the immolation of a sacrificial victim, and impose these forms on an action which is not in itself a sacrificial rite.

The last supper was not a sacrifice; it was a ritual meal at which Jesus declared the meaning of his impending death. His followers continued to gather for such a meal, and they would borrow from the language of sacrifice in order to interpret the meaning of that meal and its relationship to the cross. They would start running into trouble when the old sacrificial cultic activity began to reshape the ritual. At this point secondary symbolism—that is, the actions and procedures surrounding the concept of animal sacrifice—began running counter to the origin and intent of the eucharist.

Two very important theological developments greatly affected the evolution of ritual symbolism: the church's reaction to gnosticism, and the orthodox reaction to arianism. Chapter 1 talked about the gnostic tendency and its appearance in the earliest days of christianity. This tendency, the first heresy and the heresy that has never really ceased to threaten the christian message, wants to do away with the humanness of Jesus, his finiteness, and make him a god appearing in human form but not really subject to the finite human condition. Gnosticism disdained the world of flesh and matter; so the only body the son of God could have without contaminating himself was an apparent body.

In order to defend the doctrine of the incarnation, orthodoxy had to defend material creation itself. In the area of worship, this led to an increasing emphasis on the material elements of bread and wine, and the objects and exterior actions of the ritual.[15] Ancient sacrificial rites and the rites of the mystery cults provided a ready-made set of cultic ideas for carrying out this emphasis. Thus, at the end of the second century, Irenaeus would speak of the bread and wine as *offerings*.[16] A simple idea like this had far-reaching consequences. Formerly the bread and wine had simply been brought to the table; now they were not only brought but "offered to God." The preparation of the bread and cup became the "offertory." The act of worship which had been known mainly as the eucharist, the "thanksgiving," came more and more to be called the "offering" or the "sacrifice." Presiding celebrants became known as "priests." And the eucharistic table, which had never been important as an object, came to be seen as an "altar" because on it the victim was offered. Christians were once opposed to tables of stone, which suggested pagan sacrifices; by the middle ages, so thoroughly had sacrificial symbolism taken over that stone altars (or at least an altar stone) were formally required.

There were positive sides to this development. For example, along with the idea of the bread and wine as an offering made to God came the practice of bringing gifts to the altar. The symbolism here could be very rich, and it is retained in the blessing prayers of the new roman rite. The bread and wine, along with whatever other gifts are brought forward, are "the fruit of the earth and the work of human hands." Thus is the whole of creation, including our lives and our labor, offered to God the creator and goal of creation. But this aspect of sacrificial symbolism presupposes the engagement of the faithful in the eucharistic action. This activity was destined to diminish as a result of a second theological development, namely the orthodox reaction to arianism.

Arianism put Christ the Word in a platonic netherworld between God and man. Orthodoxy insisted that if Christ is to be the savior of mankind and the reconciliation between God and man, he must be thought of as one in substance with the Father. A century later emphasis would have to be put on his being equally one in substance with mankind. But in the meantime, throughout the fourth and fifth centuries, there was an increasing awe for the divinity of Christ and fear at approaching the holy table where his most sacred mysteries were celebrated. The language of fear and awe became common in sermons. Church architecture, ceremonial and liturgical prayers all emphasized Christ's distance from man (a curious reversal of the central meaning of the incarnation), and communion gradually ceased to be understood as an integral part of christian worship. The anti-arian development came during the centuries after christianity had become a legal religion, an event which brought about much adaptation to and influence from the culture at large. The church's liturgical symbolism may well have been influenced by the rites of the mystery religions, which stressed the secret and the awesome. There are strong overtones of this influence in the baptismal and eucharistic instructions of this era.[17]

The combined reactions to gnosticism and arianism cannot of course be isolated from the many other social and cultural factors which influenced christianity and its self-understanding during these five centuries. But the combination is significant. First came emphasis on the material elements of worship, and a much too facile accommodation of old cultic symbolism to the primary symbolism of eucharist, thanksgiving. But the elements were, so to speak, still in the hands of the faithful, who still had a place in the "offering of the sacrifice." Then came an emphasis on the sacredness of the act, which finally moved the objects and the activity surrounding them away from the faithful.

Eucharistic *theology,* as we read it in the church fathers, still had its roots in the biblical tradition and was often extremely rich. But the eucharistic *liturgy* and the liturgical practice (or non-practice) of the faithful was moving in another direction. The objectification of the bread and wine was not formalized until after the patristic era; as I mentioned in chapter 4, Radbert's ninth-century treatise is the first extant document which makes the eucharistic question a question about the bread and wine "out there" on the altar table. But the liturgical symbolism of the fourth and fifth centuries already contained a focus on objects, with an overlay of old cultic symbolism, which would later divide eucharistic theology in two: a theology of the real presence, and a theology of sacrifice which abstracted from the participation of anyone but that of the celebrant. Hearing bishops like Ambrose and Chrysostom complain about the large number of people who communicated only once or twice a year or never, one can guess that the eucharist had already become an object "out there" for a great many of the faithful long before theology adopted the same position.

But there is one extremely important factor in the patristic way of seeing material reality which continued to protect the eucharistic theology of this era. People were not yet in a position to distinguish the empirical question from the symbolic question. It was assumed that anything real was symbolic, that any object out there was a symbol of something hidden, something *more* real, something still to come. Since no distinction was made between the empirically "real" and the symbolically "real," we have to be careful how we interpret the "realistic" language of the church fathers.

In fourth- and fifth-century writers like Cyril of Jerusalem, Ambrose, Chrysostom and Theodore, there are a good many expressions referring to a change or transformation in the eucharistic elements, to something happening at the words of institution. Their language was most vivid, and that vividness extended to every detail of the rite.

Theodore of Mopsuestia, for example, wanted his flock to see the death and resurrection of Jesus played out in the eucharistic ritual. When the bread and wine are brought out, we are to imagine that Christ is being led out to his passion. Placing the offerings on the altar completes the representation of the passion, and "from now on we should consider that Christ has already undergone the passion and is now placed on the altar as if in a tomb." All of this takes place in silence because "when our Lord died, the disciples also withdrew for a while in a house in great recollection and fear." With such dispositions we watch what is being done because "at this moment Christ our Lord is to rise from the dead, proclaiming to all a share in his sublime blessings." At the invocation of the Holy Spirit, by whom Christ was once raised from the dead, the dead body of Jesus becomes his risen body. The bread is finally broken and given out in communion "just as our Lord shared himself out in his appearances, appearing to different people at different times, and finally to a great gathering. In this way everyone was able to come to him."[18]

We would hardly be inclined to carry secondary ritual symbolism quite this far (liturgical reform has done away with similar medieval interpretations of the roman rite). But we must also appreciate what Theodore is trying to do. He sees the connection between the eucharist and the cross, and he affirms it much more simply in other places. But he also exploits secondary sacrificial symbolism in order to relate the present to the past. Still more important for him is the future: the earthly liturgy, which re-enacts the past in the present, is also a symbol of the heavenly liturgy and the future existence that awaits the christian people. Eating the bread which is the Lord, "with great delight and joy and in strong hopes, we are led in this way to the greatness which through the resurrection we hope to experience with him in the world to come."[19]

Theodore therefore works his symbolism at three levels: the present action is related both to the past and to the future. All three levels are evoked in the following statement, a typical interpretation of primary meaning through secondary cultic symbolism:

In every place and at every time we continue to perform the commemoration of this same sacrifice; for as often as we eat this bread and drink this chalice, we proclaim our Lord's death until he comes. Every time, then, there is performed the liturgy of this awesome sacrifice, which is the clear image of the heavenly realities, we should imagine that we are in heaven. Faith enables us to picture in our minds the heavenly realities, as we remind ourselves that the same Christ who is in heaven, who died for us, rose again and ascended to heaven, is now being immolated under these symbols. So when faith enables our eyes to contemplate the commemoration that takes place now, we are brought again to see his death, resurrection and ascension, which have already taken place for our sake.[20]

Within the patristic context, this is a superb statement of the meaning of the eucharist. What distracts us today is the expanded imagery of sacrifice, for we no longer practice cultic sacrifices; at best we simply know of them historically, and at worst we associate them with some sort of magic. Kaesemann makes a significant point in asserting that if we have any concern for the clarity of the gospel and its intelligibility to the present generation, theological responsibility compels us to abandon the kind of sacrificial interpretation which began developing with the Letter to the Hebrews.[21]

But this should also warn us how to interpret patristic statements about what "happens" to the bread and wine at the words of institution. We have inherited the language of "change" in this connection, a language which does not mean to us what it meant to the church fathers. They do *not* shift from the symbolic to the empirical level (as we are inclined to do) when they make statements about the bread and wine "becoming" the body and blood. Their language of change and moment of change is radically symbolic, and indeed associated with *secondary* eucharistic symbolism. Such language does not appear historically—and I would maintain *could* not appear— until the cultic ideas of oblation and sacrifice had expanded into a dramatic rite surrounding the breaking of the bread.

Moreover, even after the language of change came into use, it was never isolated from the ceremony and applied to the bread and wine alone. What is said of the *participants* goes hand in hand with what is said of the *elements*. Leo the Great once used the easter passover theme to stress this connection. If our food and drink is the Lord himself, the important thing is that sharing this food "makes *us* 'pass over' into what we receive, so that everywhere we carry him with whom we are dead, buried and raised to life."[22] John Chrysostom is even more vivid. Through the food the Lord has given us, we become "members of his flesh and of his bones," we are "mixed into" that flesh, and he has "kneaded his body with ours."[23] This rather carnal symbolism might not appeal to the modern mind. But the point is that such symbolism must be taken right along with the fathers' language about change in the elements of bread and wine.

So long as secondary symbolism had not cut loose from the primary and become independent of it, such symbolism could reinforce the primary. The imagery of Leo and Chrysostom, for example, builds on the original pauline image of the body of Christ. When Paul warns the corinthians that they are eating and drinking their own condemnation because they have failed to "discern the body," he has several notions of "body" in mind. He is referring not just to the eucharist and the risen Lord, but above all to the *ecclesial* body of Christ which figures so prominently in Paul's writings. Much as Theodore sees the "sacrifice" of Christ in three dimensions—past, present and future—so the fathers see the "body of Christ" at the same three levels: the body of Jesus dead and raised up, the body of the church (head and members) as it is now, and the body of the church as it is destined to become. All three bodies are signified by and celebrated in the eucharistic action, which thus intersects present, past and future.

Augustine explained it this way in one of his easter sermons: The bread and wine which you see on the altar, sanctified through the word of God, are the body and blood of Christ. If you receive worthily, "you are what you have received." You are to "become bread, that is, the body of Christ" because "in that bread you are taught how you ought to value unity." The bread was made from many grains ground together, mixed with water, baked with fire: you were ground by your lenten penance, baptized with water, anointed with the fire of the Holy Spirit. This "being what you have received" is what Paul meant when he said that as the bread is one, so we though many are one body. The eucharistic sacrifice is therefore "a sign of what we are," because Christ "wished us also to be his sacrifice." This is why after the eucharistic prayer, after the "sanctification of the sacrifice" is completed, we say the Lord's Prayer and embrace one another with a sign of peace. Our hearts are to be with our brothers, just as our lips have touched them. We then eat the body of Christ. But is the body of Christ eaten? No, it is not consumed. The church of Christ, the members of Christ who are now cleansed, will one day be crowned. So what is signified in the body that is eaten will last eternally, even though it seems to pass.[24]

Augustine thus expands the original pauline "body of Christ" by adding further liturgical symbols. He also brings in the idea of sacrifice, and he makes statements about the elements of bread and wine. The primary pauline meaning, though expanded through secondary symbolism, remains the same and is in fact reinforced. Augustine cannot speak of the eucharistic body without speaking of the body which is the church; the one does not make sense without the other. Both together explicate the meaning of the historical body and blood given for the forgiveness of sins: we are to seek unity, become one just as the bread is one, in order one day to join our head where he has gone.

Unfortunately the richness of this theology was not to be sustained. Secondary symbolism was also sacralizing the liturgical action itself, and the gradual removal of the faithful from any active part in the ceremony would eventually take its toll. During the last half of the first millennium, the meaning of "body" changed.[25] For as the faithful no longer saw themselves as an essential part of the eucharistic body, the *ecclesial* meaning of body was lost and an essential link was broken.

Theology would now have to find some other way to link the bread and wine with the historical body of Jesus or with a heavenly body. Heavily physical notions of real presence and sacrifice were the way found, and perhaps the only possible way.

As for the church, it was no longer seen as the fathers saw it: a eucharistic community, a faith community which receives and expresses its identity in the breaking of the bread. The church would now become primarily a legal body, a "perfect society" like the state, and juridical concepts would take over from the theological concepts that were lost. That is a very important point omitted in the nostalgic sketch at the beginning of this chapter. For along with the liturgical reform of the past decade has come more and more resistance to legalism in the church, and to any conception which would define the church mainly as a juridical body. Such resistance is eucharistically well founded.

7

From Magic to Mystery

IN OUR GROWTH as persons, our personal past history feeds into and shapes what we are now, what we have become. We might reject what we have done in the past, undergo a change of heart, follow a new course; but we never throw off our past. This is a truism, but it always bears repeating because it has profound consequences for us. If some important stage of personality development whereby a child learns how to relate to others is shortcircuited in infancy or adolescence, this will naturally affect how the person behaves as an adult. Everyone has short circuits of some kind, and the constant challenge for an adult is to understand what he has become, know what his resources are and what they are not, and how to rally the resources he possesses to meet his own and others' needs. The forgiveness of sin gets its religious importance from the fact that our past includes sinfulness which affects our present resources. The forgiveness of sin does not negate the past; it says that whatever the past may have been, this does not matter now. Go in peace, knowing that you are accepted by God not just despite your past but *with* your past.

The gospel message is a promise of a new future, a future that has broken in upon us in the person of Jesus. But a tension regarding the value of the past runs through all the New Testament writings: the "fulfillment" accomplished in Jesus involves continuity as well as discontinuity with what went before. The same tension occurs in our own experience of religious conversion, and it is what makes conversion difficult to live out. Conversion involves a change of heart, a determination to take a new direction. But that direction is taken from where one stands now, with everything his past has made him—happily and unhappily.

Our religious past tells us much about the present and about the stages we go through in interpreting the meaning of God, religion, and all the concepts tied up with religion. The development of religious practice and understanding from primitive times to our own is of course a complex story. For the purposes of this chapter, the story can be schematized into three stages:

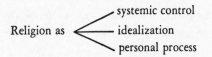

Religion as ⟨ systemic control / idealization / personal process

Each stage is exemplified both by the history of mankind's religious development, and by our individual personal development.

Religion as systemic control. The consciousness of primitive man was completely tied up with what goes on in the world of nature.[1] God, man and nature were all indistinct, undifferentiated in man's perception of reality. There was one single energy or animating principle pervading everything, a "soul-substance" forming a bond between man and animals and the crops. Animals and plants constitute man's food supply, and primitive man's religious concerns revolved around his search for food. His rituals were means of renewing and keeping "charged" the productivity and fertility of nature, and thus of enabling the community to preserve its life and to control the unpredictable.

Animals and plants shared the same sacred energy as man, and this made nature both helpful and dangerous. Men chose animals to be their guardian spirits because of the animal's particular characteristics (the eagle, the fox, the serpent, the bear). But this created problems because animals also provide food for man. Killing any animal whose soul-substance was tied up with the individual or the tribe called for an appropriate ritual. If animals were eaten, this had to be done with respect and reverence and due apology. Certain animals, especially those who were guardian spirits for the whole community, were too sacred to be eaten at all; and yet the inherent vitality or soul-substance of the guardian spirit had to be imbibed. This was often accomplished by a ritual sacrifice once each year. It is the giving of life rather than the taking of life that is important here. The outpouring of an animal's blood established a bond between man and what he saw as the supernatural order, between man and the mysterious uncontrollable world that provided him with food.

A more settled agricultural society gradually came to replace the tribes who lived by hunting alone (a development not unlike that of the famous american wild west, when the cowboys and cattlemen had to come to terms with the farmers who were putting up fences and roping off the land to protect their crops). With the dawn of agriculture, the meaning of religion did not change; man, God and nature were still quite undifferentiated. The food supply had to be maintained, and yet the soul-substance inherent in the crops made them dangerous unless they were approached with due solemnity and apology. The first-fruits of the earth had to be offered to the deity if they were to be eaten with impunity, and the life-giving energy contained in the newly reaped grain had to be ritually transmitted back to the earth, so that the guardian spirit would not take revenge and withdraw from the processes of growth.

We thus find primitive religion dealing with three basic elements: ritual *impulsion* of soul-substance into nature, so that animal and vegetative processes could remain charged with energy; ritual *expulsion* of any demonic forces which might interfere with these processes; and *control of taboos,* so that animals and crops could be eaten without injury either to the eater or to the productive forces of nature itself.

Systemic control reached an extreme in the practice of human sacrifice. The aztecs of Central America required a perpetual round of human sacrifices to enable the sun to continue its daily course across the heavens and thus ensure the fertility of the crops. The extraction of hearts from human victims who represented the gods kept the gods alive ("the god is dead, long live the god"). In this way the powers of nature were kept alive and enabled to perform their functions. African tribes, too, made human sacrifices in order to guarantee the fertility of the land; the ritual pouring of human blood into the ground invested the earth with vitality. Head-hunting and ritual cannibalism are related forms of systemic control. Soul-substance resides especially in the head, and the head-hunters' villages needed this vital energy in order to guarantee fertility. As for cannibalism, its purpose was to imbibe the soul-substance of the deceased in order to gain possession of his vital energy. Moreover, imbibing the vitality of the person whom one has killed forms a sacred bond which prevents the ghost of the dead man from doing any injury.

It is easy for modern man to write off such practices as gross and extreme, or at least hopelessly naive. This is to forget that at least some of these practices or variations on them are inevitable so long as God, nature and man remain undifferentiated in man's consciousness. A two- or three-year-old child's concept of God is not distinguishable from his concept of mother or father or whatever other people supply him with what he needs, reward him when he has done the right thing, and punish him when he has done something wrong.

As a child grows older, he is taught to pray. His first prayers are bound to deal with such things as asking for a bike for his birthday. For all of us, prayer begins as a means of systemic control. If I get my bike, I have said the right prayer or performed the right ritual; if I don't get it, something was lacking in my prayer. As I grow older, I realize that the correct performance of a ritual does not guarantee control over the system. But this realization comes only as I grow up. (And the old practices die hard: deep down I still feel that the right prayer will help my team win the championship game.) Morality does not come into play until much later. Prayer, worship, God and mother and dad are initially all wrapped up with reward for saying and doing the right thing, rejection or punishment for saying or doing what this mysterious pack of authorities defines as wrong. At this stage I don't yet understand "right and wrong." All I know is what brings me satisfaction and what does not. The fact that my big sister is going to have an expensive wedding next month, or that my little brother has fewer toys than I do—this does not yet matter to me and my birthday bike. These are negative forces that can be repulsed if only I perform the right ritual. The right prayer, the right words, the right behavior is bound to bring me what I want.

A child needs to go through the stage of magic, of not stepping on the cracks in the sidewalk, just as mankind had to work its way through attempts at ritual control of the fields and flocks. The difficulty is that adult man has shown himself quite capable of reverting to this stage where religion is basically systemic control. When this happens, faith in God is indistinguishable from faith in any of the systems that surround us. We all know about the american dream and the whole conception of America as the land of opportunity. "Anyone who does a good day's work will succeed." Straightforward magic is involved here, and it is little different from the primitive notion that the correct performance of a ritual will guarantee fertility and productivity.

When christians revert to this stage of religious awareness, the church is little different from any other system or institution. It has its own internal structure and method of government, but basically it reinforces the status quo and lets the devotee know that the systems do work and will continue to work. A "religious person" will here be defined largely as one who goes to church on sunday. But even for the so-called non-religious person, such things as a church wedding or the baptism of one's children will be most important. The church and what it says about God is indistinguishable *from* God, and indeed from the other processes of nature and society. So to ignore the most basic and socially accepted rituals of the church is to invite trouble. There may be no faith-commitment, no follow-up for the baby who was baptized or for the couple who exchanged their consent before a christian community instead of a justice of the peace. But to ignore such rituals would be to violate basic systems and thus to invite some unknown punishment.

Punishment is a very important concept at this stage of religious understanding, because the deity is here seen mainly as one who rewards and punishes. Salvation itself comes from Jesus' having won approval by paying the required pound of flesh to a wrathful God. Working out our own salvation means keeping the commandments and doing all the things that guarantee divine approval. Heaven and hell, ultimate approval or ultimate rejection, are strong preoccupations at this stage. Resurrection from the dead has no relation to the christian idea of life *out of* death; at this stage it will mean the ultimate *reward* of life *after* death. As for suffering, this is a punishment sent by God, a punishment which would not have come had there not been some violation of the system. This attitude is exemplified by Job's friends who argued that his sufferings were at the very least a punishment for sins he had committed unwittingly or out of weakness. It is exemplified by one of the characters in the film "The Emigrants" who understood the death of his only child as a punishment for his having been too attached to the child.

Thus, while God might be quite fully personified at this stage and not *consciously* identified with the powers of nature, he nevertheless remains quite undifferentiated from other systems. He is conceived as one who works according to the patterns of cause and effect observed in the natural world—like Leibniz's great Orderer who sees to it that sins carry their punishment with them "by the order of nature" or "by virtue of the mechanical structure of things." Orsy has given a good example of a similar conception, once common in catholic moral theology, which saw God operating according to rigid systems of reward and punishment more typical of primitive societies than of a modern civilized state. A young delinquent might be guilty of a serious crime, even murder, and yet no civilized state inflicts the death sentence on minors. Modern jurisprudence recognizes the fact that it takes time to become an adult who can be held fully responsible before the law. Yet classical moral theology was able to hold that once a child reaches the so-called age of reason, somewhere around seven years, he is capable of making a radical and fully responsible break with God. "To push this reasoning to its logical limits, such moral theology believes in a God who is willing to let the child, the work of his hands, be destroyed forever whenever this child, with full deliberation and knowledge, commits a mortal sin. No legal system with a grain of humanity would authorize or permit such sanction under any circumstance."[2]

Reversion to this early stage of religious consciousness is of course very common, and no culture or christian denomination is exempt from the phenomenon. Such reversion is even very tempting. We like recipes, definite precepts and rituals which will unfailingly produce a desired effect. This tendency is deeply imbedded in us, it provides a simple and clear explanation for everything, and it will remain with us so long as people are people. Christians, however, are not to indulge in the tendency. Jesus' scathing attack on the formalism and ritualism of the pharisees implies that once a higher stage of religious consciousness is reached, certain kinds of reversion are totally destructive. There is really no place here for a theology of the

Spirit or for "discernment of the Spirit" as a fur
of the interior life. Religion as systemic control
to do with that wind which "blows wherever
tell where it comes from or where it is going" (Jn 3.8,
tendencies to regress to the level of the systemic are probably on
reason why the theology of the Spirit has remained relatively un-
developed in the christian tradition.

Religion as idealization. As human consciousness develops, man
becomes more aware of his own interiority, of the life-energy and
capacities within himself, energy which he is now able to distinguish
more clearly from the forces surrounding him. This brings a change
in religious understanding, one which is well exemplified by the
"mystery cults" of the greco-roman world. Nature and the processes
of nature still had to be conserved and promoted, but now the emphasis shifted to man himself. It is man who is to experience the full
fertilizing powers of the Earth Mother, both in this life and in the
hereafter. Immortality, the ultimate form of vitality, here emerges as
a primary religious preoccupation.

The mystery cults were all based on the death and resurrection of
a god-hero (a Dionysus or Orpheus or Osiris) who successfully
struggled with the forces of evil and passed through the doors of
death into immortal life. The experiences of these divine heroes were
ritually re-enacted, and those who took part in the rites were assured
of immortality in union with the deity. We possess few details about
the way these rituals evolved historically or how they were carried
out, but the main outlines are clear. As E. O. James summarizes it,
they were "essentially *sacramental dramas* in the sense that they offered to all classes the promise of a blessed hereafter, and aimed at
producing inner and mystical experiences calculated to quicken the
religious life of the initiates through *outward and visible portrayals
of the passion and triumph of a divine hero.*"[3]

The mystery cults thus "humanized" the ancient search for abun-
dant life; nature's cycle of birth, death and rebirth was personalized

ınd idealized in the person of the god-hero. There is an awareness here that the individual must move toward personal autonomy if he is to have any kind of self-determination and freedom. The possibility of such autonomy arises once man begins to realize that his own inner energies are not identified with the energies of the outside world, even though the energies remain related. This awareness opens the way to conception of a more personal deity. But the mystery cults do not reach full interiority. The emphasis is on contemplation of the ideal, not on personal engagement in the process that leads to the ideal. The sacred drama is contemplated from the outside, even with a great deal of emotion; but it is not yet lived from the inside.

This stage of religious development is as important for us personally as it was for mankind historically. We have to go through a process of identifying with heroes and contemplating ideals before we can appropriate ideals and make them our own. This of course is a basic human truth. There is no way our inner strengths and resources can be tested by the fire of experience unless we have first recognized, through idealization, *which* strengths and resources make the battle worthwhile. One of the very important functions of religion, therefore, is to present an ideal with which one can identify. (I should point out that throughout this chapter, whenever I talk about individual experience of the three stages, I am choosing my examples from christian and sometimes specifically catholic experience. The same principles apply outside christianity, but the symbolic forms will be different.)

At this stage one's concept of God changes, and the change is a very refreshing one from the God of systemic control, God the Enforcer. At this stage, as the contemporary christian experiences it, God is Love, and Jesus is the perfect lover of God and man. The "mythologized Christ" is very important here, that is, all of the comforting and inspiring imagery created around the risen Jesus: he is the new Adam, the new man, the new creation, the ideal toward which the entire cosmos is moving. I suspect it was no accident that the thought of Teilhard de Chardin, which developed this type of imagery and made it acceptable to contemporary man, appealed so strongly to catholics at a time when they were beginning to raise questions about formalism in the church. For many, Teilhard provided an exciting and even scientifically interesting means of working a transition from the stage of systemic control to idealization (and beyond; Teilhard by no means stops short with idealization).

At this level of experience worship is or can be a strongly emotional experience (some styles of worship are too incessantly dull to be able to exploit this stage of religious development). It is especially in the liturgy that the sacred drama is contemplated, a drama that is enhanced by all the colors and sights and sounds of the ritual action. The sacraments are no longer basically rites that must be performed to keep the systems working and to ward off possible evils. Now the sacraments become identification with Christ the hero, involvement in ideal love, the great "yes," an affirmation of commitment to the gospel way of life. *Commitment* is a very prominent idea at this stage, and it is enforced by the strong feelings that regularly accompany worship here. (But dark shadows loom up from time to time, suggesting that commitment *to* the gospel might not be quite the same thing as engagement *in* the gospel. Am I really committed if I don't always *feel* my commitment? How am I going to say yes, and what is my yes going to mean, if ever these positive, reinforcing feelings go away?)

This is a very necessary stage of religious development, and we all repeat it from time to time. We can easily recall the times in our lives when idealization and all the religious attitudes that go with it have been primary forces in our lives. We can also confirm from personal experience that a return to this stage is an entirely different thing from reverting to the first stage. The trouble is, this stage is so *comfortable* that we are reluctant to move on. A good many christians want the church to remain right here, and their wishes are granted by a great deal of preaching. Tell me about the love of Christ, and give me a reassuring message to help me through the coming week; but for heaven's sake don't make me shake hands with the fellow next to me whom I don't even know. Sermons are supposed to be about God, not about politics or social welfare. I have been redeemed by the cross, and I am committed to Christ who promises me immortality. This is what I want to hear, and a preacher has no business telling me how I ought to get involved in social movements. The church is the place I go to find God and hear about God's love for me, not about other people's problems.

That caricature is rather strong, but not untypical; for at this stage, religion is still very much an individual matter between me and God. Morality is no longer mainly obedience to the commandments for the sake of an eternal reward; sin is now seen as an offense against a loving God, and one tries to live up to the ideal that is contemplated. But there are other people out there, and they have not yet seriously entered my whole conception of religion. They have not yet become an integral part of my pursuit of a relationship with God. I will love my neighbor in order to *show* my love for God, but at this stage my neighbor is not part of my notion of a union with God. He has his union, I have mine.

The difficulty of moving beyond the stage of idealization is exemplified by people's reactions to the gospel stories about Jesus. Christians are terribly threatened by the fact (and it is a fact, not a theological theory) that the life of Jesus as it is narrated in the gospels follows the same pattern as countless other ancient stories about hero-gods: a miraculous but humble birth, a rapid rise to prominence, a triumphant struggle with the forces of evil, a betrayal and death and final vindication through some sort of immortality. As I tried to emphasize in chapter 1, what is unique about christianity is Jesus, not the way his story is told. This is precisely the point that cannot be grasped unless one goes beyond the stage of idealization and tries to find out what the stories are saying about human experience. The stories about Jesus are hero-stories recounting a sacred drama. The problem is whether the drama is going to be merely looked at or also lived. Many people are deeply moved by the story of Jonathan Livingston Seagull; but being able to *recognize* the marvels of taking flight and becoming free does not mean that one has thereby *done* it.

What is very easily forgotten at the stage of idealization is that when we are all wrapped up with looking at the ideal, we are also compromising with it. Or at least, compromise is all that is left for us if we never move beyond the stage of idealization. "Compromise" is the only concept we have for interpreting our failures to live up to an ideal we observe in our heroes, in *someone else*. But at the next stage, the ideal has to become a personal interior reality, not a beautiful something-outside-me but rather something which is beautiful because it has taken a unique shape *within me.* And the trick is that the ideal I manage to realize within me never looks at all like what I once thought it would look like. If one moves beyond idealization, there will be no need to compromise with an abstraction. There will only be the need to realize that one has much further to fly.

Religion as personal process. This is the stage where death and resurrection become an interior part of our personal histories, not just a process carried through on our behalf by someone else. The transition to this stage brings with it a new attitude toward suffering and conflict and the unexpected—or rather, it is in this stage that one painfully *acquires* a new attitude toward such experiences. This is illustrated by the story of Job, who refuses to accept his friends' arguments that suffering is a punishment from God or a mere call to repentance. Job emerges from his trial with no easy answers to the problem of suffering; in fact he has fewer answers than ever before. But he is now aware that the experience of suffering has deepened him and even changed the meaning of trust in God for him. The same point is stressed by the prophet Ezekiel, who moves far beyond the view that the nation's exile in Babylon is a punishment for sin;

he sees the nation's sufferings as an occasion for conversion, interior growth and a new self-understanding. At this stage of development, suffering is no longer a thing to be tolerated and, so far as possible, held at arm's length. Suffering now has to be dealt with, appropriated in an interior way and understood as a necessary part of becoming a person. One will therefore no longer be content with contemplating the fact that God is love. Now the *meaning* of a loving God has to be coped with, in the face of all the conflict that arises when we begin taking other people seriously as *other*.

Formerly, religion was largely a matter of my personal relationship with God; now other people become an integral part of my personal religion. Love of God and love of neighbor used to be fairly separate questions; now, terrifyingly, the one is all wrapped up with the other. The whole God-question comes up for grabs and one is forced to rethink the whole thing: Who is God? Where is he? Who is Jesus? At this stage death to self starts to become more than a notion. The process begins to take place, really and often painfully, as we come to terms with other persons as truly other. Grace and the risen life therefore acquire a new meaning, for it is at this stage that one begins to understand experientially and not just notionally the sense of life coming *out of* death.

There is strong resistance to entering this stage and living in it. The transition from systemic control to idealization is reasonably natural, and certainly comforting. But a firm line, difficult to cross, divides idealization from personal process, because now the sacred drama has to be lived and not just looked at. Peter wanted to pitch tents and prolong the experience of the transfiguration. "Rabbi, it is wonderful for us to be here." The disciples were already perplexed at Jesus' remark about his having to suffer and die; and after the transfiguration they began to discuss what "rising from the dead" could possibly mean (Mk 9:2-10). Like them and like Jesus himself, we have to find out, by dropping below the line and entering the personal process of death and resurrection.

systemic control

idealization

———————————————

personal process

Above the line, the transfiguration and the comfort of the mythologized Christ is sufficient. Below the line, the experience of the man
Jesus becomes a pressing question. Why were all those inspiring
hero-stories told about him in the first place? Why was he given the
name that is above all names?

Above the line, one will be content to explain the divinity of
Christ by appealing to his pre-existence as the second person of the
blessed trinity. Below the line, this explanation of why Jesus is
proclaimed Lord becomes distant and unreal—as unreal as any other
explanation of things which appeals to a world we do *not* experience.

Above the line, the concepts of grace and resurrection are quite
reassuring in themselves; they are also generally indistinguishable
from the blessed immortality guaranteed by the mystery cults. At this
level one will normally be content with the explanation that such
things are "mysteries which we must accept on faith." Below the
line, any concept unrelated to concrete human experience loses its
content, and one will begin to question seriously any religious idea
that sounds suspiciously unreal or unrelated to the finite human condition.

Above the line, it is enough to know that Jesus died to save us
from our sins, and to be identified securely with that death through
baptism and occasional renewal of one's commitment. Below the
line, one has to work out the process of rising to new life by accepting responsibility for oneself as Jesus did.

Above the line, the "will of God" is something out there, something I can find by turning my gaze in the right direction. Below the
line, the will of God is a process, something which I discover only by

coming to terms with myself, who I am and what I have become, what my resources are and what they are not.

The institutional church is made up of people who live at every stage of religious development, and of people like you and me who are frightened at the thought of dropping below the line and living there. Institutions therefore do not drop below the line; people do. But if the gospel has been preached only as systemic control or at best idealization (often enough because people want it that way), religion will very often be abandoned as one moves into adulthood. The process of *human* development goes on as people (not all, but many) become socially and ethically concerned and engaged in "meeting the other." But religion is often abandoned in the process because it is no longer a viable interpretation of human experience; it has nothing to do with the process of becoming a person. The sacred drama, once so meaningful, slips away into another world; or rather, it never gets brought from that other world into *this* world. Jesus is in heaven with his glorified body and the heavenly liturgy goes on, but what is that to me? I am sorry, but all your talk and promises of immortality will not do anymore.

The feelings and emotions associated with the stage of idealization recede as one enters the stage of personal process, and the old images and symbols are no longer the comfort they used to be. With this stage's emphasis on interiorization, public worship will be abandoned unless it is seen as a social action, an action which expresses a communal quest for meaning and a communal coping with the process of suffering and growth. In short, at this stage the "body of Christ" becomes more than a sacred object to be contemplated. If it does not, and if preaching and liturgical practice have not restored the ecclesial meaning of the eucharistic body, this sacrament will be as irrelevant as the rest of religion. It will be just one more of those beautiful incense-clouded symbols which a mature adult looks back on with fond memories of the time when idealization worked.

Above the line, faith in Jesus is basically faith in an outsider. Below the line, one comes to know the Jesus in whom one believes.

Faith is now fully an assent to the presence of God in one's own *personal history,* and this assent is quite indistinguishable from hope. The faith and the hope is this: that to engage in the process that went on in Jesus is to know God and find union with God. At this stage one begins to understand the death-exaltation symbolism of John, and some of those wild statements of Paul which sound beautiful but make little sense at the stage of idealization: "The Spirit of God has made his home in you," and "if the Spirit of him who raised Jesus from the dead is living in you, then he who raised Jesus from the dead will give life to your own mortal bodies through his Spirit living in you" (Rom 8:9-11). Resurrected life is no longer some vague immortality or life after death, but the wholeness of life that comes *out of* death in any form. It is an integration of flesh and spirit, a type of life which we touch upon and discover in single experiences of death to self.

Christian ritual, particularly the eucharist, will be saying something quite new at this level—the only level where the idea of expectation and future hope makes fully human sense. Celebrating the eucharist once expressed commitment to an ideal; now it expresses a search for integration, the hope that such integration is personally possible, that my own history will lead to wholeness. Once the eucharist celebrated the drama of Jesus, not yet my own drama. Now it celebrates something of my own and proclaims a death I have begun to understand.

Christian worship celebrates the process that mystics like Saint John Eudes saw as necessary if we are to make any sense of that phrase we use so glibly: the "mysteries" of Christ's life.

Since your duty is to continue and fulfill in yourselves the life, virtues and actions of Jesus Christ on earth, so must you also prolong and fulfill, in yourself, the states and mysteries of Jesus, and frequently implore Jesus himself to consummate and accomplish them in you and in his whole church.

You cannot too often realize and reflect on the truth that the mysteries

of the life of Christ have not yet reached their full perfection and complete-
ness. Although they are perfect and complete in Christ's own person, they
are not yet completed in you who are his members. . . . It is the plan of
the son of God that his whole church should participate in and actually be,
as it were, the continuation and extension of the mystery of his incarnation,
birth, childhood, hidden life, public life of teaching and of labor, his passion and his death, by the graces he desires to impart to you, and by the effects he wishes to accomplish in you through these same mysteries. By this
means, he desires to fulfill his mysteries in you.[4]

But such language, like all religious language however inspiring, can
only lead us to the line where religion becomes personal process. The
"mystery of Christ" can never be anything more than a beautiful
and elaborate puzzle until the process is engaged in.

8

Sacrifice

THE IDEA OF SACRIFICE has been floating in and out of these pages, and it has not yet been dealt with adequately. It is a troublesome idea which complicated the history of the eucharistic ritual and eventually led to divisions in the western church. And yet we continue to speak of the "eucharistic sacrifice," of "altars" and "priests" and all the trappings of ancient sacrificial cults. What does the idea mean?

A few years back, catholic journals and newspapers and letters to the editor were putting the question this way: Is the mass a meal or is it a sacrifice? Much of the debate was prompted by the fact that the catholic tradition of recent centuries did not really possess a theology of the *eucharist*. There was, as I have noted in several contexts, a theology of the real presence and a theology of the sacrifice of the mass. But as the liturgical changes of the 1960's were introduced, it became painfully evident that the two theologies were inadequate for interpreting the developments that were taking place.

Protestant theology was in no better shape to deal with the idea of eucharist as sacrifice. Protestant positions on this idea had been formulated in reaction to medieval abuses, and the concept had virtually dropped out of their theological vocabulary. Ecumenism and the need to re-evaluate positions taken four centuries ago have made both sides deal with theological inadequacies and blind spots in their interpretations of the idea of sacrifice.[1]

In one sense the meal-sacrifice debate can be resolved quite simply. The concept of *meal* answers the question "What are we doing?" The eucharist is and always was a ritual meal; it was intended to be, but not always was in fact, a meal in which all the faithful share. The concept of *sacrifice* answers the question "What do we mean by what we are doing?" This meal proclaims the saving death of the Lord, the sacrificial act which reconciled man and God. So there is no need for any conflict between the two concepts.

But this solution is somewhat too neat. Chapter 6 pointed out some of the serious problems that developed as sacrificial symbolism was gradually worked into the eucharistic ritual, which was not in its origins a rite of blood sacrifice. It is all very well to say that the sacrifice of the mass is in every way the same as the sacrifice of Calvary, except that it is unbloody. This same idea brought with it (inevitably?) a whole package of secondary symbolism which eventually squeezed the laity out of the ritual action and quite thoroughly changed the shape of the eucharist. We are now in a position to remove the accretions of secondary cultic elements which are not natural to the eucharistic action. Much of this has in fact been done.

Hindsight tells us much about how christian worship and its symbolic forms *ought* to have developed. But if Jesus is new, and if in the breaking of the bread we are celebrating a new thing, we are also tied up with the old. The religious forms and symbols of the pre-christian era are part of our collective history. Our psyche continues to supply us with the past and with our most human roots, and there is simply no way for us to expect the future or reach for it apart from symbols we have inherited from our collective past. This is why it is and has been possible for christianity to make use of past religious *forms* without necessarily reverting to past religious *consciousness*.

A good example of this is the development of the liturgical year. For perhaps a century after the death of Jesus, sunday was the only christian feast. This was the Day of the Lord when the faithful met for worship, strongly aware that in breaking bread in memory of the risen Lord they were looking forward to that final Day when the new creation would be realized. During the first century there does not even seem to have been a feast of easter, that is, a time of the year which commemorated the historical event of Jesus' death and resurrection. The liturgical cycle was based on the week, not on the year. Four centuries later the picture looked quite different. Sunday retained its importance, of course; but there was now a fully developed cycle of feasts and seasons commemorating the events recounted in the New Testament. By the fifth century, in other words, the historical *past* had acquired an importance which it did not have for earlier christians.

Scholars have evaluated this development in different ways. There are dangers inherent here, some of which I have already mentioned. If one's only model for interpreting the easter event is the historical sequence known as Good Friday—Easter Sunday—Ascension Thursday, the resurrection of Jesus can easily come to mean simply life after death: he picked up with a glorified body where he left off with an ordinary body. The liturgical scheme, if it is treated as straightforward history, will also have little relationship to our own personal histories—to our own experiences of death, resurrected life and the coming of the Spirit into our lives.

Further problems arise if the idea of commemorating the *past* leads to a loss of the *future* dimension of the liturgy. The eucharistic action proclaims the death of the Lord "until he comes." It is a sacrament of union and reconciliation accomplished in Jesus, but not yet accomplished *in us*. If this orientation toward the future, this theme of expectation and hope is forgotten, christian worship simply becomes a matter of present and past. When this happens, the liturgical cycle draws us into an eternal repetition of events which, however meaningful and comforting they may be, really lead us nowhere. At christmas we think of how nice it is that there was at least one peaceful, peace-bringing event in history. We think of how nice it would be if there were more of the spirit of this beautiful season in the world, this season of good cheer and twenty-four-hour ceasefires. At easter we are reassured that Christ came out of the tomb, that spring is coming, that the lilies still bloom. Period. In this perspective the past reassures us and makes the present tolerable. As for the future, there will always be another christmas, another easter, an endless cycle to comfort us and give meaning to the passage of time, while we go on living pretty much as we always have.

This attitude toward christian worship, where it exists, is of course a complete reversion to primitive cyclical religion, where religious experience was completely undifferentiated from the cycle of nature, and where the cyclical re-enactment of sacred dramas made the "terror of history" tolerable. Primitive man found himself powerless against any kind of flood or famine or natural disaster, the misfortune of war or the injustice built into the rigid codes of ancient society. The regularity of sacred feasts and seasons enabled him to put up with these terrifying irregularities.[2] But *tolerating* suffering and conflict is not the same as *appropriating* suffering and conflict as a necessary part of the "personal process," the process of human and religious growth. Where interiority is lacking, the liturgical cycle commemorating the life, death and resurrection of Jesus is nothing more than idealization. It is a comforting story that enables one to hold the question of personal engagement in this process—the personal "terror of history"—at arm's length.

I keep repeating phrases like "when this happens" or "where this attitude exists." This does happen of course in the case of people for whom religion is mainly a sociological thing. It happens with those for whom religion and worship consecrate the status quo, the search for the good life, people who are disturbed by anything which upsets the present order of things or by anyone who challenges that order. Many church-goers are quite content with the present and the past. The liturgical cycle recreates the inspiring life of Jesus, and the mass re-enacts the beautiful saving act of Calvary. As for the future, it will surely be a magnification of the present, a divine reinforcement of the same cycle that enables assistant vice-presidents to become first vice-presidents and eventually presidents.

But anyone reading these pages already knows the many uses to which religion can be put. For all the distortion that is possible here, it is much too simplistic to say (as not a few scholars have said) that the idea of an annual liturgical cycle is merely a christian takeover of pagan feasts of sun-gods and nature-gods, for the sake of accommodation to the mentality of the age. Something far more basic is going on here. For one thing, christians live between the past and the future, between the coming of Jesus and the coming of Jesus. The symbolism of worship tries to express this—not always successfully, because any symbols which attempt to create an intersection between past, present and future are eminently subject to distortion in one direction or another. One need only think of the "real presence" where that presence is quite reduced to the *present* with little relation to the past *or* the future.

Despite all the distortions and formalism that always had to be corrected, the hebrews very naturally took over fertility rites and nature feasts, reinterpreting them in accord with their own religious experience. Christianity did the same thing in a different cultural context. What the hebrews did with mesopotamian and canaanite culture, christians did with the greco-roman culture. One liturgical scholar has observed that what is astonishing about the christian liturgical year is not that it developed so slowly, over a period of four or five centuries, but that it developed at all; for every celebration of the eucharist is a celebration of the life, death and resurrection of the Lord.[3] On the contrary, I think it would have been astonishing if christianity had *not* eventually restructured the time of the year and given a new meaning to the passage of time, however superficial that meaning might have become with the further passage of centuries. The psychological needs and religious insights of primitive man are not abolished by a new religious insight, even if the new experience transcends the old.

I have elaborated on the problem of the liturgical cycle at some length because this example shows things we need to watch for in evaluating the symbolism of blood sacrifice. Such symbolism is woven through the whole New Testament interpretation of the death of Jesus, and it was very naturally attached to the eucharist before the end of the first century. Now if problems eventually developed at the altar, what about the cross itself? What does it mean to call *the cross* a sacrifice, and how has this been understood?

There is no need to give a long list of New Testament passages which evoke the ancient world of ritual sacrifices. In addition to John's symbolism which we have looked at, there is Paul's and that of others. We are redeemed, bought back for God by the blood of Christ, paid for in the blood of the Lamb, redeemed in Christ Jesus who was appointed by God to sacrifice his life so as to win reconciliation for us. Here as elsewhere, numbness sets in because we have heard such words so often. But how are they to be understood? What is such imagery saying about the event of Calvary? The interesting thing is that the christian tradition has understood the atoning act of the cross at *all* of the levels of religious consciousness outlined in the last chapter.

Some of the church fathers developed interpretations in line with the negative force of ancient blood rituals, where blood was understood to ward off evil forces. According to this view, the offering made on Calvary satisfied the devil's rights; it was a ransom paid by the god-man to Satan in order to rescue the world from his clutches.

Other interpretations fell in line with the positive aspect of blood rituals, where the outpouring of a victim's blood kept the systems of nature charged with vitality. In line with this view, Satan had no rights, and mankind did not need to be "ransomed" from the devil; it was the rights of God that were vindicated and "satisfied" on Calvary. The first interpretation runs through the theology of the patristic era, and the second is that of Anselm and many medieval scholastics.

Both of these interpretations of the sacrifice of Calvary operate at the level of systemic control. That is, a blood sacrifice performed by a representative of the human race is needed in order to expiate guilt, bring the cosmic system back into balance, and guarantee the supply of vitality from God to man. The idea of "grace" here has close affinities to the soul-substance of archaic religion, if one were to push the "ransom" and "satisfaction" theories to their logical conclusion. In this view, moreover, the redemption of mankind is quite exclusively the activity of Jesus; there is a definite passivity on the part of the christian. The various theories of vicarious substitution, in which Jesus is the god-man paying a debt owed by a guilty race, opened the way to theological interpretations which would place a wide gulf between the initiative of Jesus and the christian's personal response to that initiative. Many aspects of the controversy over faith versus good works flow from a rather systemic view of the redemptive act of Christ.

Some of the church fathers resisted this line of interpretation. Gregory of Nazianzus wrote that there was no satisfaction paid either to Satan *or* to God because there was no question of mankind's being held captive. Gregory's explanation appeals to a very sophisticated concept of the divinity as something, someone, who is made fully manifest in the man Jesus. "The Father accepts the sacrifice, not because he demanded it or needed it, but because this was part of the divine plan, since man had to be sanctified by the *humanity of God*."[4] This line of interpretation was picked up at the beginning of the scholastic era by Abelard, who saw the death of Jesus as the supreme manifestation of the love of God, not a ransom paid to Satan or a satisfaction of the divine anger. Thomas Aquinas followed the same line of thought.

With these thinkers we get beyond the more primitive idea of sacrifice. No vicarious substitution or ritual expiation for sin is needed in this latter view of the cross of Jesus. But note that such an interpretation does not in itself solve the problem of making the transition from idealization to personal process. The saving work of Jesus can still be simply contemplated as an ideal act of love for God, an act which saves us who remain quite passive and unengaged. Or on the other hand, the action of Jesus can be reflected on, interiorized, and become an act in which we ourselves become involved.

***

What then are we to make of the whole notion of sacrifice, with all its connotations of ancient blood rituals and all the varied interpretations to which the concept has led? Earlier I mentioned Kaesemann's suggestion that fidelity to the gospel message in our time might mean doing away with sacrificial interpretation in an age when people have no experience of the cult of sacrifice. This would certainly apply to secondary symbolism and the material trappings and social castes of the ancient cults: priests as sacred people, the laity as not-so-sacred people; altars and churches as divine places, streetcorners and homes as non-divine and secular places. But the basic symbolism of sacrifice has been written into christian self-understanding much too thoroughly to be written off by twentieth-century criticism, despite whatever distortions might have come out of this symbolism. Whatever one does with the *ritual accouterments* of sacrifice, the *conception* of sacrifice has to be dealt with. If sacrifice can mean, as it does mean in everyday parlance, everything from giving up candy for lent to doing something truly noteworthy for someone else, then we are inevitably going to *symbolize* this archetypal concept in our worship. The concept is not going to be detached very easily from the death of Jesus or from the eucharist simply because we are removed from the old order of blood sacrifices. The idea of sacrifice—the giving of life to promote and conserve life—remains in us in radical psychic forms.

James makes the interesting observation that where sacrificial symbolism ceases to operate "the associated religious order tends to disintegrate." At the time of the reformation, protestantism shifted the emphasis from the eucharist to the atonement, from the altar back to the cross. Eventually the idea of sacrifice disappeared almost totally except as a purely subjective offering of a pure heart. Any external symbolization of this offering, through the symbolism of sacrifice, came to be seen as unfaithful to reformation principles. James concludes that this break-up of the old ritual order was one of the most important causes of the modern collapse of institutional religion.[5] Whether or not one can put this much weight on sacrificial symbolism alone, it is certainly true that the fear of over-externalizing has often stripped protestant worship of all color and human feeling.

The problem lies not in *using* the symbols of sacrifice and altar and priesthood, but in *how* we use them. Understanding of the sacrificial idea will go hand in hand with one's understanding of salvation, resurrection, immortality, and the atoning act of Calvary itself. *All* of these concepts, as I have tried to emphasize, are understood differently at the different stages of religious consciousness—both historically and personally, both by catholics and by protestants.

If one reads the idea of sacrifice in a systemic way, priests will be magical people ordained to control our relationship with God the Enforcer, and endowed with the power to tell even God what to do —like Joyce's priest, who spoke of the power and authority "to make the great God of Heaven come down upon the altar and take the form of bread and wine." The idea of sacrifice changes at the stage of idealization; at that stage, sacrificial symbolism enhances contemplation of the sacred drama. The patristic elaboration of the symbols of sacrifice, discussed in chapter 6, took place under the influence of idealization, and the old roman rite inherited much of this emphasis. Finally, at the stage where religion becomes personal process, the understanding of sacrifice must become truly interior. Protestantism rejected sacrificial symbolism in the very good interests of interiorization; but this led to an unrealistic rejection of externals and of the very positive contributions of the stage of idealization. And if catholicism has sometimes reverted to the magical understanding and ritual formalism of the systemic stage, protestantism has also frequently returned to non-ritual aspects of that stage, where God is one who rigorously rewards and punishes and rigidly predestines. (*All* christians share reversions to stages of religious consciousness where none of us should be. The only way for us, the western church, to cut through our scandalous divisions is to admit where we have been, recognize that where we have been is human enough, and move on again to the death-resurrection process in which we are all supposed to be engaged.)

A thoroughly christian and interiorized notion of sacrifice is possible. As Augustine develops it in the *City of God*, sacrifice becomes a concept which expresses the whole meaning of christian interiority and its relation to worship. Augustine is aware that sacrifice has always been associated with the worship of God. But as we have learned from the prophets, God is not benefited by sacrifice. Ritual offerings are symbolic of what goes on in man's heart, symbolic of the true sacrifice he makes of *himself* as he "dies to the world in order to live for God." True sacrifices are the works of mercy done for ourselves or our neighbor, the same works of mercy in which we find our own peace and happiness. Our bodies themselves are a sacrifice, as Paul suggests when he tells us to worship God by "offering your living bodies as a holy sacrifice pleasing to God" (Rom 12:1). The symbol of *sacrifice* thus links up with the symbol of *body*. Since the true sacrifice of works of mercy is our means of finding happiness and belonging to God, "it follows that the whole of that redeemed city, that is, the congregation or communion of saints, is offered as a universal sacrifice to God through the High Priest who, taking the form of a servant, offered himself in his passion for us that we might be the body of so glorious a head."

It is therefore we ourselves who constitute the whole sacrifice, all of us with the different gifts and graces we bring to the love and service of our neighbor.

Such is the sacrifice of christians: "We, the many, are one body in Christ." This is the sacrifice, as the faithful understand, which the church continues to celebrate in the sacrament of the altar, in which it is clear to the church that she herself is offered in the very offering she makes to God.[6]

The key to Augustine's interiorization of sacrifice, and the link between the altar and the cross, is the ecclesial body living for God. It is this ecclesial, social reality which gives reality to the sacrificial symbolism applied to the eucharist. With this ecclesial understanding of the body of Christ, Augustine is able to exploit the old cultic symbols:

Christ Jesus is both the priest who offers and the oblation that is offered. And it was his will that as a sacrament of this reality there should be the daily sacrifice of the church, which, being the body of him, her head, learns to offer itself through him. This is the true sacrifice of which the ancient sacrifices of the saints were but many and manifold symbols.[7]

Another age would see in this passage an interpretation of the eucharist, plain and simply. But here as above, the "sacrament" and "daily sacrifice" refer not just to the rite but even more importantly to the church, the living sacrifice without which the eucharist is *unintelligible* as sacrifice.

Sacrament, body of Christ, sacrifice—in Augustine's hands these ideas and images are all ways of spelling out the meaning of the church and the kind of personal process its members are called to engage in. I mentioned earlier how the notion of "body of Christ" was evacuated when its ecclesial meaning was forgotten. The same thing applies to "sacrifice."

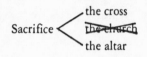

With the living sacrifice missing, one is left with an exterior cult which at best represents the sacrificial drama of Calvary (idealization) and at worst magically reproduces it (systemic control).

But the notion of "church" is no different from the other religious ideas discussed in this book. Until religion becomes a personal process, the church will be understood as merely a system or an ideal. In giving a title to this book, I was tempted to write *Jesus, the Church, the Eucharist*. But I felt this would have been misleading, because the word "church" as we normally use it does not yet make most of us think of a living sacrifice, a personal process writ large. Maybe it will be difficult ever to grasp the magnitude of such an idea. It is quite enough to deal with the personal process writ small. This involves keeping hold of the core of our faith, and seeing to it personally and in our own small communities that our rites and symbols express the core rather than pull us away from it: God is not first to be found out there, in temples on Twelfth Street or Pleasantview Avenue, but in the temple of our hearts. What was once outside is now within, so that finding God and worshiping him is completely tied up with finding ourselves.

Notes

Chapter 1: Flights into magic

1. See P. Schoonenberg, *The Christ* (New York: Herder, 1971), pp. 50-188.

2. Here and elsewhere in this chapter, I am borrowing some of the materials I used in my article, "The Scandal of the Cross," *The Way* 13 (1973) 33-40.

3. This is Lonergan's summary of F. Heiler's analysis of common characteristics in these world religions. See B. Lonergan, *Method in Theology* (New York: Herder, 1972), p. 109.

4. Justin, *First Apology*, chaps. 21-22.

5. For an excellent introduction to this fascinating area of knowledge, see C. G. Jung (ed.), *Man and his Symbols* (London: Aldus, 1964; New York: Dell Laurel edition). Part 1 on approaching the unconscious and Part 2 on ancient myth and modern man are especially useful. A well-organized collection of interesting ancient texts can be found in J. Henderson and M. Oakes, *The Wisdom of the Serpent: The Myths of Death, Rebirth and Resurrection* (New York: Collier, 1971). Joseph Campbell's *The Hero with a Thousand Faces* (Princeton/Bollingen, 1949) is a classic.

6. Penguin edition, pp. 158-159.

Chapter 2: Two questions about reality

1. This idea is effectively developed by Jan Groot, "The Church as Sacrament of the

World," in *The Sacraments in General,* vol. 31 of the *Concilium* series (New York: Paulist, 1968), pp. 51-66.

2. S. Langer, *Philosophy in a New Key* (3d ed.; Harvard, 1957), chap. 10. My treatment of the "two questions about reality" relies heavily on the philosophy of sign and symbol developed by Mrs. Langer. Chaps. 2-6 are particularly useful for sacramental theology.

3. *Ibid.,* p. 291.

4. A. Haden-Guest, "The Ubiquitous Sound of Muzak," in *Insight,* sunday magazine of the *Milwaukee Journal* (March 4, 1973), p. 27.

5. Cyril, *Baptismal Homilies,* 2; trans. E. Yarnold, *The Awe-Inspiring Rites of Initiation* (London: St. Paul Publications, 1971), p. 76.

6. J. Cirlot, *A Dictionary of Symbols* (New York: Philosophical Library, 1962), p. xxviii, p. 8.

7. Leibniz, *Discourse on Metaphysics,* 89. Italics mine.

8. St-Exupéry, *The Little Prince* (New York: Harcourt Brace, 1943), pp. 96-97 (Harbrace paperbound).

Chapter 3: The last supper and the eucharist

1. Translation abridged and modernized from *The Authorized Daily Prayer Book,* ed. Hertz (New York: Bloch, 1948), pp. 965 ff.

2. Dom Gregory Dix, *The Shape of the Liturgy* (London: Dacre Press, 1945), chap. 4. Research done since 1945 enables us to nuance a number of Dix's points, but his whole treatment of the last supper remains one of the most insightful ones I know of; the entire book shows unusual sensitivity to the many facets of christian liturgical history. For a more recent (and very detailed) explanation of the jewish liturgy, the blessing prayers, the development of the eucharistic prayer, and eucharistic developments during the middle ages and the reformation, see Louis Bouyer, *Eucharist* (Notre Dame, 1968).

3. A. Jaubert, *The Date of the Last Supper* (New York: Alba House, 1965), p. 96.

4. A. Dupont-Sommer, *The Essene Writings from Qumran* (New York: World, 1962), pp. 108-109.

5. *Didache,* 9.

6. E. Stauffer, *Jesus and the Wilderness Community at Qumran* (Philadelphia: Fortress, 1964).

7. *Constitution on the Sacred Liturgy,* par. 10.

8. See J.-J. von Allmen, *The Lord's Supper* (Ecumenical Studies in Worship, no. 19; London: Lutterworth, 1969), pp. 42-43. This book is one of the best and most readable works on eucharistic theology which has appeared in the past decade. The author's treatment of various ecumenical questions (intercommunion, priesthood, pluralism of understanding) is particularly outstanding.

Chapter 4: The bread and wine

1. On the origin of *sacra* and sacraments, see Langer, *Philosophy in a New Key,* chap. 6.

2. E. Schillebeeckx, *The Eucharist* (New York: Sheed & Ward, 1968), p. 59. Except for

this point, the first chapter of this book is a valuable historical study of what the Council of Trent did and did not say.

3. J. McCue, "The Doctrine of Transubstantiation from Berengar through the Council of Trent," *Harvard Theological Review* 61 (1968) 385-430. The same article is published in *Lutherans and Catholics in Dialogue, III: The Eucharist as Sacrifice* (published jointly by the U.S. Catholic Conference and by the U.S.A. National Committee for Lutheran World Federation).

4. *Ibid.*, pp. 429-430.

5. An excellent survey of this development can be found in J. F. Powers, *Eucharistic Theology* (New York: Herder, 1967), pp. 111-179.

6. Useful historical surveys of the medieval developments can be found in Bouyer, *Eucharist* (see above, chap. 3, note 2); see also E. Schillebeeckx, *Christ the Sacrament* (London: Sheed & Ward, 1963), chap. 3, and appendix to chap. 2.

7. See Langar, *op. cit.*, chap. 4, on the difference between presentational and discursive symbols. For a good appreciation of the many non-verbal aspects of worship, read Marianne Micks, *The Future Present: The Phenomenon of Christian Worship* (New York: Seabury, 1970).

Chapter 5: The cross and the eucharist

1. This difference in "mental and physical standpoint" is developed by D. W. Wead, *The Literary Devices in John's Gospel* (University of Basel, 1970), chap. 1.

2. I am much indebted to C. H. Dodd, *The Interpretation of the Fourth Gospel* (1st ed. 1953; Cambridge paperback, 1968). Dodd's analysis of johannine sources in the first part of his book is now out-dated, but his treatment of the argument and internal structure of the gospel (pp. 289-453) remains one of the most insightful studies available. See also O. Cullmann, *Early Christian Worship* (London: SCM, 1953); though Cullmann has been criticized for pushing johannine "sacramental" symbolism too hard, his study nonetheless calls attention to symbolic elements that cannot be overlooked in the gospel as it stands.

3. A very readable study of the development of worship in ancient Israel, with many interesting suggestions for contemporary worship, is that of Walter Harrelson, *From Fertility Cult to Worship* (New York: Doubleday, 1970).

4. Translated from the french edition of Ephraim's *Commentary on the Diatessaron*, in *Sources chrétiennes*, vol. 121, pp. 110-112.

5. In the following paragraphs I am borrowing from my article, "The Challenge of Christian Faith," in *The Way* 11 (July, 1971) 192-201.

6. Dodd, *op. cit.*, p. 439.

7. *Ibid.*, pp. 434-435.

8. Leo the Great, *Sermon* 70, 4-5.

9. G. Scholem, *Major Trends in Jewish Mysticism* (New York: Schocken, 1951), p. 27.

Chapter 6: Symbol upon symbol

1. John H. McGoey in *Homiletic and Pastoral Review* 61 (1960-61) 541-547.

2. Quoted in *HPR* 60 (1959-60) 353.

3. Fr. Ginder in *Our Sunday Visitor*, February 2, 1964.

4. *Ibid.*

5. *Acta apostolicae sedis* 49 (1957) 425-426; Instruction *Inter oecumenici* (Sept 26, 1964) n. 95; Instruction on the Worship of the Eucharistic Mystery (May 25, 1967) nn. 53-55.

6. Dix, *Shape of the Liturgy*, p. 412, 419.

7. This theme was developed especially by dutch theologians during the 1960's and is closely linked with the debate over "transignification." See Powers' survey and summary (reference above, chap. 4, note 5).

8. C. Vollert summarizes this curious debate in *Theological Studies* 22 (1961) 391-425.

9. Dodd, *Interpretation of the Fourth Gospel*, p. 437. It is remarkable that Raymond Brown's commentary on John's gospel in the Anchor Bible series makes no allusion to the liturgical meaning of *telein* in greek literature.

10. Dix finds two strata discernible in the development of eucharistic prayers, *op. cit.*, pp. 214-237.

11. Austin Farrer, "The Eucharist in 1 Corinthians," in *Eucharistic Theology Then and Now* (London, 1968).

12. Dix, *op. cit.*, p. 232.

13. *Ibid.*, p. 234.

14. *Didache*, 14; *1 Clement*, 36, 40-44.

15. See J. Jungmann's excellent summary of this development, "The Defense against Gnosticism," *The Early Liturgy to the Time of Gregory the Great* (Notre Dame Press, 1959), chap. 10.

16. Irenaeus of Lyons, *Adv. Haer.* 4.17.5.

17. See E. Yarnold, *The Awe-Inspiring Rites of Initiation* (London: St. Paul Publications, 1971), pp. 50-62.

18. Theodore, *Baptismal Homilies*, 4.25-26, 28-29; 5.11-12, 17-18 (Yarnold, pp. 227 ff.).

19. *Ibid.*, 5.18 (Yarnold, p. 249).

20. *Ibid.*, 4.20 (Yarnold, p. 224).

21. E. Kaesemann, *Jesus Means Freedom* (Philadelphia: Fortress, 1970), p. 114.

22. Leo, *Sermon* 63.7.

23. Chrysostom, *Homilies on John*, 46.

24. Augustine, *Sermon* 227. Augustine has traditionally been considered a "symbolist" in contrast to "realists" like Ambrose. This distinction, which comes out of the eucharistic disputes of the 9th and 11th centuries, does not seem to me to stand up under examination of the texts. Augustine does not carry his secondary symbolism as far as some of the other fathers do, and so his symbolism sounds less "physical." The question here is one of *degrees* of secondary symbolism, not of difference in symbolic mentality.

25. H. de Lubac, *Corpus Mysticum* (Paris: Aubier, 1949).

Chapter 7: From magic to mystery

1. For an excellent survey of the development of sacrificial ritual and the concept of sacri-

fice, see E. O. James, *The Origins of Sacrifice* (London, 1933; reissued by Kennikat Press, 1971). J. G. Frazer, *The Golden Bough*, contains a goldmine of historical data (Macmillan, 1922; abridged paperback edition, 1963). I am indebted to one of my students, Dennis Blaser, for some of the summaries I have used in this chapter.

2. L. Orsy, "Communal Penance: Some Preliminary Questions on Sin and Sacrament," *Worship* 47 (1973) 341.

3. James, *op. cit.*, p. 138. Italics added. For a provocative study of man's interpretations of death and the question of immortality, see John Dunne, *The City of the Gods: A Study in Myth and Mortality* (New York: Macmillan, 1965).

4. John Eudes, *The Life and the Kingdom of Jesus in Christian Souls* (New York: Kenedy, 1946), p. 251.

Chapter 8: Sacrifice

1. For a fine example of how ecumenical dialogue is carried on at the theological level, see the volume of *Lutherans and Catholics in Dialogue* cited above, chap. 4, note 3.

2. This is the central theme of Mircea Eliade, *Cosmos and History: The Myth of the Eternal Return* (New York: Harper & Row, 1959). The author develops the difference between cyclical religion and judeo-christian faith.

3. Cyrille Vogel, cited by T. Talley, "History and Eschatology in the Primitive Pascha," *Worship* 47 (1973) 212.

4. Gregory Naz., *Orations*, 45.22.

5. James, *op. cit.*, pp. 288-289.

6. *City of God*, 10.6; Image edition (Doubleday, 1958), pp. 193-194.

7. *Ibid.*, 10.20 (p. 196).